Suicide Bombers

Suicide Bombers

Titles in the Lucent Terrorism Library include:

THE
LUCENT
TERRORISM
LIBRARY

Suicide Bombers

Debra A. Miller

LUCENT BOOKS

An imprint of Thomson Gale, a part of The Thomson Corporation

THOMSON

GALE

Detroit • New York • San Francisco • San Diego • New Haven, Conn. • Waterville, Maine • London • Munich

© 2007 by Lucent Books. Lucent Books is an imprint of The Gale Group, Inc., a division of Thomson Learning, Inc.

Lucent Books® and Thomson Learning™ are trademarks used herein under license.

For more information, contact
Lucent Books
27500 Drake Rd.
Farmington Hills, MI 48331-3535
Or you can visit our Internet site at http://www.gale.com

LIBRARY OF CONGRESS CATALOGING-IN-PUBLICATION DATA

Miller, Debra A.
  Suicide bombers / by Debra A. Miller
    p. cm. — (The Lucent terrorism library)
  Includes bibliographical references and index.
  ISBN 1-59018-748-2 (hard cover : alk. paper) 1. Suicide bombers—Psychology.
2. Suicide bombings — Prevention. 3. Terrorism—Prevention. I. Title. II. Series.
HV6431.M572 2006
363.325—dc22

                2005037305

Printed in the United States of America

Contents

Foreword

It was the bloodiest day in American history since the battle of Antietam during the Civil War—a day in which everything about the nation would change forever. People, when speaking of the country, would henceforth specify "before September 11" or "after September 11." It was as if, on that Tuesday morning, the borders had suddenly shifted to include Canada and Mexico, or as if the official language of the United States had changed. The difference between "before" and "after" was that pronounced.

That Tuesday morning, September 11, 2001, was the day that Americans began to learn firsthand about terrorism, as first one fuel-heavy commercial airliner, and then a second, hit New York's World Trade Towers—sending them thundering to the ground in a firestorm of smoke and ash. A third airliner was flown into a wall of the Pentagon in Washington, D.C., and a fourth was apparently wrestled away from terrorists before it could be steered into another building. By the time the explosions and collapses had stopped and the fires had been extinguished, more than three thousand Americans had died.

Film clips and photographs showed the horror of that day. Trade Center workers could be seen leaping to their deaths from seventy, eighty, ninety floors up rather than endure the 1,000-degree temperatures within the towers. New Yorkers who had thought they were going to work were caught on film desperately racing the other way to escape the wall of dust and debris that rolled down the streets of lower Manhattan. Photographs showed badly burned Pentagon secretaries and frustrated rescue workers. Later pictures would show huge fire engines buried under the rubble.

It was not the first time America had been the target of terrorists. The same World Trade Center had been targeted in 1993 by Islamic terrorists, but the results had been negligible. The worst of such acts on American soil came in 1995 at the hands of a homegrown terrorist whose hatred for the government led to the bombing of the federal building in Oklahoma City. The blast killed 168 people—19 of them children.

But the September 11 attacks were far different. It was terror on a frighteningly well-planned, larger scale, carried out by nineteen men from the Middle East whose hatred of the United States drove them to the most appalling suicide mission the world had ever witnessed. As one U.S. intelligence officer told a CNN reporter, "These guys turned airplanes into weapons of mass destruction, landmarks familiar to all of us into mass graves."

Some observers say that September 11 may always be remembered as the date that the people of the United States finally came face to face with terrorism. "You've been relatively sheltered from terrorism," says an Israeli terrorism expert. "You hear about it happening here in the Middle East, in Northern Ireland, places far away from you. Now Americans have joined the real world where this ugliness is almost a daily occurrence."

This "real world" presents a formidable challenge to the United States and other nations. It is a world in which there are no rules, where modern terrorism is war not waged on soldiers, but on innocent people—including children. Terrorism is meant to shatter people's hope, to create instability in their daily lives, to make them feel vulnerable and frightened. People who continue to feel unsafe will demand that their leaders make concessions—*do something*—so that terrorists will stop the attacks.

Many experts feel that terrorism against the United States is just beginning. "The tragedy is that other groups, having seen [the success of the September 11 attacks] will think: why not do something else?" says Richard Murphy, former ambassador to Syria and Saudi Arabia. "This is the beginning of their war. There is a mentality at work here that the West is not prepared to understand."

Because terrorism is abhorrent to the vast majority of the nations on the planet, President George W. Bush's declaration of war against terrorism was supported by many other world leaders. He reminded citizens that it would be a long war, and one not easily won. However, as many agree, there is no choice; if terrorism is allowed to continue unchecked the world will never be safe.

The volumes of the Lucent Terrorism Library help to explain the unexplainable events of September 11, 2001, as well as examine the history, personalities, and issues connected with the ensuing war on terror. Annotated bibliographies provide readers with ideas for further research. Fully documented primary and secondary source quotations enliven the text. Each book in this series provides students with a wealth of information as well as launching points for further study and discussion.

Suicide Terrorism: A Growing Threat

One of the most frightening trends of the new millennium is the phenomenon of suicide terrorism. In the typical suicide attack, explosives are strapped to the attacker's body or packed into a car that the attacker drives. When the explosives are triggered, the attacker dies along with the target. Increasingly, the targets are innocent civilians. Common in other countries since the early 1980s, suicide terror first struck inside the continental United States on September 11, 2001. Unlike the typical suicide attack, however, the terrorists on 9/11 did not use explosives. Instead, in a spectacular plan, they turned commercial aircraft into giant bombs, ramming the planes into skyscrapers in New York City and the Pentagon in Washington, D.C., and killing themselves along with almost three thousand civilians. The event sparked a global U.S. "war on terrorism" and changed the way Americans think about security in their everyday lives. Once blessed by a feeling of national invincibility against the kind of violence that is a fact of life for people in places such as Israel, people in the United States suddenly realized that they, too, might be similarly vulnerable. Today, shed of their illusions of safety, a majority of Americans believe that another terrorist attack on America is possible.

Yet suicide terror tactics are not a completely new phenomenon. As early as the eleventh century, a radical sect of Muslims called the Assassins murdered princes, generals, and civilians from a rival sect. They did not attempt to flee; instead they allowed themselves to be killed as part of their missions. In the late nineteenth century, anarchists opposed to the czarist system of government in Russia assassinated czarist leaders, often killing themselves at the same time. And in World War II, Japanese kamikaze pilots became famous for suicide missions in which their airplanes were loaded with explosives and used as flying bombs to strike enemy ships and other targets.

Modern suicide terrorism did not develop until the 1980s, when it was introduced in the Middle East by Iran and an Iranian-supported Islamic group in Lebanon called Hizballah. Soon, suicide tactics spread to nearby Palestinian groups who used them against Israeli civilians throughout the 1990s and into the present decade. Probably everyone in the United States has seen the television images showing the carnage wrought by Palestinian suicide bombings of Israeli buses, shopping malls, and restaurants. In recent years, this type of terrorist violence has spread around the world, as extremist groups in places as diverse as Sri Lanka, Russia, Kashmir, Indonesia, Morocco, Israel, and Pakistan have embraced suicide bombs as their weapon of choice.

Indeed, suicide attacks have both increased in number and become much

A car bomb detonates in Jerusalem. Terrorism by explosive devices is a daily fact of life in parts of the Middle East.

more lethal in the last few years. Experts who study suicide terrorism count 462 suicide attacks between 1980 and 2003, with the vast majority occurring since 2000. Also, according to a 2003 congressional report, although these suicide attacks made up only 3 percent of the total terrorist attacks worldwide during this period, they accounted for almost half of all terrorist-inflicted deaths during that same time. In 2004, the last year for which data are available, total terror attacks around the world tripled, rising from 175 in 2003 to 651 the following year, according to statistics released by the U.S. government. Government statistics did not separate out suicide attacks, but experts say the numbers of suicide attacks also grew rapidly in 2004.

Most of the recent increase in suicide attacks can be attributed to fundamentalist Islamists; they now form the fastest-growing suicide terror threat. Al Qaeda—the Islamist terror group that claimed responsibility for September 11 and other suicide terrorism against the United States—is the leader in recent suicide terror, conducting more than one hundred suicide attacks since 2000. Al Qaeda plans very carefully in order to pull off sensational attacks that will exact the highest number of casualties. Al Qaeda has also branched out, forming a loosely connected global network that has carried out multiple, coordinated attacks spanning countries and even continents. Since 2001, for example, groups suspected of connections with al Qaeda have carried out successful suicide attacks in Indonesia, Kenya, Pakistan, Morocco, Turkey, Saudi Arabia, Spain, Britain, Jordan, and Iraq. Today, Iraq is fast becoming the center of the world's Islamist terrorism: Al Qaeda–affiliated insurgents there are conducting multiple attacks each day against both U.S. forces and Iraqi civilians. In addition, extremist groups not directly affiliated with al Qaeda, but inspired by its fundamentalist Islamic rhetoric and its anti-America, anti-Israel, and anti-West messages, are planning and executing suicide attacks against Western targets independently.

A Japanese kamikaze pilot prepares for his suicide mission during World War II.

Emergency personnel rush to the scene of a truck bomb explosion in Iraq, which has become the center of worldwide Islamist terrorism.

Experts expect suicide terrorism to continue to mount in the future. The horrific September 11 attacks in New York and Washington, D.C., may be only the start of the violence to come. The development of new weapons and communications technology and the spread of weapons of mass destruction are expected to add to the toolboxes of terrorists, making them even more dangerous. The Internet already has been a tremendous boon to al Qaeda, allowing it to spread its violent message and tactics across the globe. Today's proliferation of weapons of mass destruction—including biological, chemical, and nuclear weapons—is an even bigger concern. Terrorist groups are known to be interested in acquiring such weapons. Unless this trend is reversed, all signs point to ever more effective and perhaps catastrophic suicide attacks in the future. Suicide terrorism truly has become a dangerous scourge upon modern society.

Chapter One

The Problem of Suicide Terrorists

Modern suicide bombings are often associated with the Middle East, particularly Israel, which has lived with a daily threat of suicide bombs since the early 1990s, when Palestinian groups began a campaign of strikes against Israeli civilians. Today, Israel remains one of the most dangerous spots for suicide terror attacks, and suicide tactics have also been adopted by insurgent groups in several other countries. In addition, in recent years, a loosely organized group of Islamic extremists and sympathizers has targeted tourist sites and other locations around the world. In some regions, suicide terrorism has become a terrifying fact of everyday life, although for most people it remains only a random, low risk. By its very nature, however, suicide terror presents a serious and growing security threat for all countries.

Israel's History of Suicide Terror

Modern suicide terror first arose in the Middle East, where the low cost and lethal effectiveness of suicide bombs made them a favorite tactic of Arab insurgent groups. The first major modern suicide bombings took place in Lebanon, an Arab country that shares a border with Israel. In June 1982, Israel invaded the Lebanese capital of Beirut to remove a Palestinian insurgent group, the Palestinian Liberation Organization (PLO), which had established a base in Lebanon in order to attack Israel. The PLO forces withdrew and an international peacekeeping force, made up of U.S., French, and Italian soldiers, was stationed in Lebanon to maintain order. This occupation of Lebanon by foreign troops, however, sparked a two-year campaign of suicide bombings by an anti-Israeli, Islamic group called Hizballah or "Party of God." Hizballah sought to oust Israeli, U.S., and other foreign troops from the country. Although civilians were sometimes killed, Hizballah's attacks were largely directed at military targets such as convoys, artillery positions, and army barracks. Hizballah's attacks ushered in a new world of suicide terrorism.

In the 1990s, nearby Palestinian groups began using suicide tactics in their struggle against Israel—a development that soon made Israel the world's most well-known site of suicide terror. These Palestinian groups have specialized in attacks on Israeli civilians, carried out by individual suicide bombers (men and women, sometimes even teenagers) who wear special belts containing explosives strapped underneath their clothing. The bombers strike by infiltrating Israeli security and then choosing a populated target inside Israel, such as a bus or restaurant, where the

Hizballah's two-year offensive of terrorism in Lebanon left many scenes such as this one in the capital city of Beirut.

The Iranian Roots of Suicide Terror

Iran has been a key player in the modern trend of suicide bombings. In 1979, an Islamic revolution brought to power a new Iranian leader, Ayatollah Ruholla Khomeini, who sought to spread a radical version of fundamentalist Islam throughout the Muslim world. In 1982, Khomeini helped to found and provided training and support for Hizballah, an Islamic group in Lebanon that became the first to use suicide bombs. In 1984, Khomeini introduced suicidal "human wave attacks" as a weapon in the Iran-Iraq War. These human waves were made up of tens of thousands of mostly unarmed Iranian children, some as young as twelve, who advanced as a massive swarm on Iraqi machine guns and positions until they either won the battle or were all killed. The Iranian suicide tactics are based on a concept of Islamic martyrdom that arose in a battle that took place thirteen hundred years ago in Karbala, a town in Iraq. The battle was fought between two sects of Muslims, Shias and Sunnis, and the Shias were all slaughtered. Among Shia Muslims throughout the Middle East, Karbala has become a symbol of self-sacrifice for the great cause of true Islam.

Ayatollah Khomeini called for Islamic revolutions throughout the Muslim world.

bomb is detonated. TV cameras routinely capture the bloody images for Western audiences. Since September 2000, more than four hundred Israelis have died in Palestinian suicide bombings and more than four thousand have been wounded.

The goal of this Palestinian terrorist violence is to force Israel to withdraw from territories it seized in the 1967 Arab-Israeli war—lands claimed as Palestinian homelands. Among the various Palestinian organizations—the PLO, Hamas, the Islamic

Jihad, and the Al-Aqsa Martyrs Brigade—Hamas is the strongest and the most lethal. Hamas's charter calls for the destruction of Israel, and the group has consistently rejected negotiations that might result in less than a complete Israeli withdrawal from all Palestinian lands. As Hamas leader Abdel Aziz al-Rantisi explained in April 2004, "Peace talks will do no good. . . . We do not believe we can live with the enemy."[1] In line with this policy, Hamas conducted a series of suicide bombings beginning in the mid-1990s designed to derail the Oslo accords, a U.S.-sponsored plan for negotiating peace between Israel and the Palestinians. Once peace talks collapsed in September 2000, sparking a violent Palestinian uprising called the Second Intifada, Hamas acquired more popular support and expanded its terrorist activities. Since 2000, in fact, Hamas is credited with fifty-three suicide attacks that killed 289 Israelis and injured another 1,649, most of them civilians.

Many Palestinians view Hamas as freedom fighters engaged in a valiant struggle

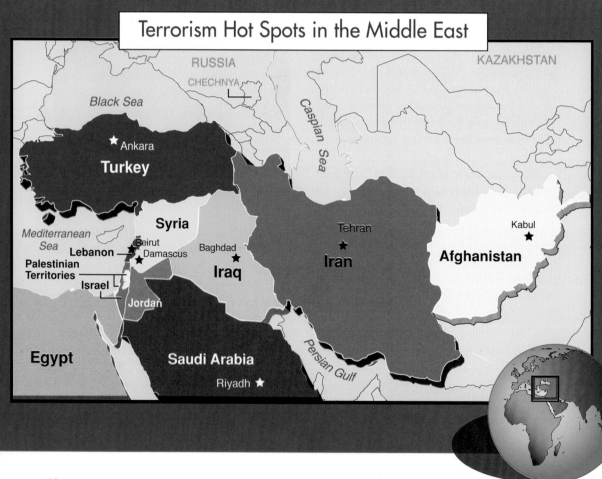

Terrorism Hot Spots in the Middle East

for an independent Palestinian state. In January 2006, Hamas candidates won a surprise landslide victory in Palestinian parliamentary elections, making the group now the legitimate, elected representative of the Palestinian people. For Israelis, however, the years of Palestinian suicide terrorism have meant lives filled with fear and pain. For the most part, people must go about their normal business, but many Israelis constantly worry about terrorist attacks and avoid large crowds or public places where attacks might be likely to occur. Many adults, for example, avoid restaurants and cafés, entertaining instead at home. For children and teenagers, the threat requires limiting social activities to visits with friends and trips to well-guarded shopping malls. As Liat Margalit, a Jerusalem teenager, explains, "Usual things that teen-agers do, we don't get to do. We don't get to celebrate our prom night, we don't get to celebrate our finals. We don't get to do anything really. It's like living in a cage."[2] In addition, children grow up fearing that they, their parents, or their siblings might die in an attack, and the entire nation suffers from depression and anxiety disorders. As radiologist Michael Messing says, "[Suicide terror] has literally affected the entire nation on a psychological level."[3]

The unlucky victims of suicide terror and their loved ones suffer the most, however. The bombs kill randomly, ripping apart families and spreading waves of grief and pain that are felt for years and even lifetimes. Those who are merely injured sometimes wish they had died. Suicide bombs are packed with nails, screws, nuts, ball bearings, and other objects that fly outward in the blast to inflict gruesome injuries. X-rays taken of victims of suicide bombings, for example, often show hundreds of metallic fragments embedded in their skin, muscles, organs, and bones. Sometimes these can be removed; other times, people must live the rest of their lives with pain from the metal shrapnel. Other common injuries from suicide bombs include amputated limbs, severe burns, bone fractures, disfiguring lacerations, paralysis, deafness, and blindness. In 2004 and 2005, the number of successful attacks sharply declined, but Israel continues to feel threatened by Palestinian terrorism today.

Sri Lanka's Tamil Tigers

Suicide tactics have also been exported to countries outside the Middle East. The group that has conducted the most suicide bombings in contemporary times is the Liberation Tigers of Tamil Eelam (LTTE or "Tamil Tigers") in Sri Lanka. This group is fighting to win independence for a minority ethnic group, the Tamils, from Sri Lanka's majority ethnic group, the Sinhalese. Between July 1987 and February 2000, a specially trained unit called the "Black Tigers" carried out 168 suicide attacks, killing more than five hundred people and injuring thousands. The Tamils' terrorism campaign is part of a savage, twenty-year-long civil war in Sri Lanka that has killed more than sixty-five thousand people and displaced more than 1.5 million.

Members of the elite suicide bomber squad known as "Black Tigers" are honored by the Tamil Tigers of Sri Lanka.

Unlike Palestinian groups, the Tamil Tigers have not targeted the civilian population of Sri Lanka but have focused largely on strategic government and military targets. As German journalist Christoph Reuter explains, the Tigers' aim is to "target with utmost precision the nerve center of the Sri Lankan state—either through attacks on decision makers or on the most susceptible weak spots in the infrastructure."[4] The Tigers carried out their first suicide operation on July 5, 1987, and over the years, they have destroyed army camps, military headquarters, and Sri Lankan oil reserves. Many attacks have also targeted politicians, both in Sri Lanka and neighboring India. One of the first high-profile Tiger attacks occurred in 1991, when a suicide bomber assassinated former Indian prime minister Rajiv Gandhi as a protest against India's involvement in the Sri Lankan war. In 1993, the Tigers struck again, assassinating the president of Sri Lanka, Ranasinghe Premadasa. More politicians were assassinated as years passed. Chandrika Kumaratunga, Sri Lanka's current president, was the victim of a Tiger suicide bomb in December 1999. She survived, but lost sight in one eye from the blast.

Even though they are not the intended targets bystanders and other civilians have often been injured and killed in Tiger attacks. A mortar and suicide bomb attack on July 24, 2001, for example, destroyed half of the planes in Sri Lanka's air force and killed twenty-one people, most of them civilians. During the 1990s, suicide terrorist attacks that killed and maimed civilians became common in Sri Lanka. As social activist Sharif Abdullah explained early in 2002, "Terrorist attacks have become so routine [in Sri Lanka] they simply aren't news anymore.... For most Sri Lankans, raised for a full generation on daily doses of terrorism and violence, the ongoing cricket matches are more newsworthy than unending stories of horror and retribution."[5]

After years of civil war marked by escalating Tamil terrorism, however, the Sri Lankan government eventually began peace negotiations with the Tigers in the late 1990s. These talks resulted in a fragile cease-fire agreement in 2002, and the suicide attacks have subsided since then.

Suicide Bombers in Russia

More recently, Chechnya, an oil-rich, mountainous region in southwest Russia, has seen the rise of suicide terrorism. Suicide attacks there are conducted by the Chechens, a Muslim group with a distinct culture that has lived in this area for centuries. After the collapse of the Soviet Union in 1991, the Chechens announced their independence from Russia. The Chechen bid for independence, however, was opposed by the Russian government, which in December 1994 sent troops to invade Chechnya in an attempt to reassert Russian rule and crush Chechen resistance. This decision initiated a bloody, brutal civil war in the region that still rages today. One of the most publicized Chechen attacks occurred in October 2002, when Chechen rebels seized a Moscow theater and held about eight hundred people hostage. The incident ended when Russian forces finally stormed the building, killing most of the rebels and more than 120 of the hostages.

Chechen fighters have also conducted more than twenty-five suicide bomb attacks since 2000, many of them fatal for unlucky civilians who happened to be nearby. In December 2002, for example, a truck loaded with explosives smashed into the headquarters of the Russian-backed Chechen government, killing about eighty people. A similar truck bomb attack on a government building in May 2003 killed fifty-nine people. In another suicide attack two days later, two women carrying bombs under their clothes blew themselves up at a religious celebration in Chechnya. The target of the bomb reportedly was Ahmed Kadirov, head of the Russian-backed Chechnya government, but he was absent; instead, twelve other people were killed. Today, the Chechen suicide attacks continue, usually directed at military targets, but often killing civilians in the process.

The Rise of al Qaeda

The world's newest wave of suicide terror is not part of any independence or nationalist movement and is not limited to any particular country or region. Some of the most

The Kurdistan Workers' Party

Between 1996 and 1999, Turkey was the site of numerous suicide bombings. These suicide strikes in Turkey were conducted by the Kurdistan Workers' Party (*Partiya Karkeren Kurdistan* or PKK), a rebel group of Kurds, a non-Arabic, Muslim ethnic group that makes up about one-fifth of the Turkish population and is also found in northern Iraq, western Iran, and parts of Syria and Armenia. The PKK sought to establish an independent Kurdish state in southeastern Turkey. In 1999, however, Turkey launched a crushing military crackdown and captured the PKK's leader, Abdullah Ocalan. At the same time, Turkey sought to win over Kurdish civilians by making capital investments in Kurdish areas, introducing social-welfare programs to improve areas such as agriculture and women's education, and agreeing to several Kurdish demands on language, cultural freedom, and educational reforms. The government's campaign led the PKK to withdraw from Turkey and to renounce armed struggle.

A displaced Kurdish family suffers the effects of Turkey's military offensive against the Kurdistan Workers' Party in 1999.

lethal suicide attacks in modern history have been carried out by al Qaeda, a group driven by a fundamentalist version of the Islamic religion and led by Osama bin Laden, a wealthy Sunni Muslim from Saudi Arabia. Al Qaeda, an Arabic name that means "the base," was originally formed in the late 1980s when a group of mujahideen, or Muslim "holy warriors," was recruited from around the world to oppose the Soviet Union's 1979 invasion of Afghanistan, a Muslim country. The United States, which opposed Russian expansionism, originally helped to finance and arm this mujahideen force.

Dramatic Attacks

Despite this U.S. aid, al Qaeda has carried out numerous dramatic attacks against the United States, other Western countries, and Muslim countries it views as corrupt or not sufficiently religious in their policies. According to terrorism experts, al Qaeda's goal is to repel Western influences and establish fundamentalist Islamic governments throughout the Islamic world. The group opposes U.S. support for Israel, U.S. attempts to influence the affairs of Islamic governments and communities, and the presence of U.S. troops in Muslim countries. As the Council on Foreign Relations describes, "Al-Qaeda believes that western governments, and particularly the American government, interfere in the affairs of Islamic nations against the interests of Muslims."[6]

Al Qaeda's suicide terror campaign began in the early 1990s, triggered, many experts say, by a decision to position U.S. troops in Saudi Arabia, bin Laden's birthplace. U.S. troops were placed there with the full permission of the ruling royal family of Saudi Arabia after Iraq invaded Kuwait in 1990. Saudi rulers allowed America to use the kingdom as a base for military operations to oust Iraq from Kuwait and protect Saudi oil. At war's end, U.S. troops remained in Saudi Arabia to help keep order in the region, angering bin Laden. Thereafter, al Qaeda was implicated in a number of terrorist strikes against the U.S. military, including a 1992 bombing of U.S. troops in Yemen, a 1993 shooting down of U.S. helicopters, and the brutal killing of U.S. servicemen in Somalia. Al Qaeda also was linked to a 1995 bombing at a U.S. military facility in Saudi Arabia and a 1996 bombing of Khobar Towers, a Saudi complex housing American soldiers. Al Qaeda operatives also struck inside the United States, in a 1993 bombing of the World Trade Center in New York City that killed six and injured over one thousand people.

In 1998, bin Laden issued a public manifesto denouncing the continued presence of U.S. troops in Saudi Arabia and calling on all Muslims to kill Americans, including civilians. He stated: "To kill Americans and their allies, both civil and military, is an individual duty of every Muslim who is able, in any country, until their armies, shattered and broken-winged, depart from all the lands of Islam."[7] Soon, al Qaeda launched a string of new attacks on American and Western targets. In August 1998, for example, the U.S. embassies in Nairobi, Kenya, and Dar es Salaam, Tanzania,

A second plane is about to strike New York's World Trade Center on September 11, 2001, in an attack coordinated by al Qaeda.

were simultaneously car-bombed. The attack in Nairobi killed 213 people and wounded an estimated four thousand and the one in Tanzania killed twelve and wounded eighty-five. Another high-profile attack was the October 2000 bombing of the U.S.S. *Cole*, a U.S. ship that was docked in Yemen. A small boat carrying two suicide bombers and explosives approached the ship, blowing a 40-by-40-foot (12-by-12m) gash in its side, killing seventeen sailors and injuring thirty-nine more.

The most deadly of all al Qaeda's suicide attacks was carried out on September 11, 2001. Nineteen terrorists commandeered commercial jets and flew them into the Twin Towers of the World Trade Center in New York City and the Pentagon in Washington, D.C. The attacks killed 2,948 people and injured hundreds more. At least two hundred people jumped to their deaths from the New York skyscrapers to escape the intense fires created in the blast. Many of the victims were firefighters and other first responders who rushed into the burning buildings to save others. Of those who survived, some suffered life-altering injuries. The economic losses ran into the billions and the attack spread fear and shock throughout America. Many compare it to the assassination of President John Kennedy in 1963; as was true of that event, most Americans will always remember where they were and what they were doing when they first heard the news of the 9/11 attack.

The 9/11 incident led to a massive U.S. military response—a military attack on al

The Islamic fundamentalist Osama bin Laden is widely believed to be responsible for the 9/11 attacks.

Qaeda training bases and government supporters in Afghanistan and, later, a war to promote regime change in neighboring Iraq. So far, no other suicide attacks have been successful inside the United States. Yet al Qaeda's campaign against the United

States and its allies continues in many parts of the world.

The Spread of Islamic Suicide Terror

Since September 11, 2001, al Qaeda has established a loose network of terrorist organizations that carries out attacks around the globe. Iraq has now become the global center of this Islamic suicide terrorism. The 2003 U.S. invasion of Iraq brought an end to the regime of Iraq's authoritarian leader, Saddam Hussein. It also opened the door to foreign Islamic extremists affiliated with al Qaeda. Hundreds have flocked to Iraq to join forces with the country's anti-American insurgency. One of the main leaders of the Iraqi insurgency, until his death in 2006, was believed to be Abu Musab al-Zarqawi, a close ally of bin Laden. Al-Zarqawi's group, Jama'at al-Tawhid wal-Jihad, which formally merged with al Qaeda in 2004, is considered a major force behind Iraq's many suicide attacks. Multiple suicide attacks now occur daily, some striking U.S. troops but most killing Iraqi soldiers and civilians. Ordinary Iraqis live in a state of terror, unable to move freely in their own neighborhoods and country and wondering if they or their loved ones will be the next victims in a suicide bomb attack.

In addition to its operations in Iraq, al Qaeda has formed strong alliances with numerous other extremist groups and individuals that have conducted numerous attacks around the world—in the Middle East, the Far East, Africa, Southeast Asia, and Europe. For example, Kashmir, an area claimed by both India and Pakistan, is the home of Islamic extremists affiliated with al Qaeda who stormed the Indian Parliament in December 2001 and have since conducted numerous attacks across the Indian border. Another al Qaeda–affiliated group, Jemaah Islamiyah, is credited with suicide attacks in October 2002, August 2003, and October 2005 that targeted locations frequented by Western tourists in Bali and Jakarta, Indonesia, killing more than two hundred people. Other incidents linked to al Qaeda include a November 2002 bombing of an Israeli-owned hotel in Mombasa, Kenya, and attacks in May 2003 on three residential compounds occupied by Westerners in Riyadh, Saudi Arabia, and on Western buildings and businesses in Casablanca, Morocco. In 2005, a car bomb attack in the Egyptian resort town of Sharm el-Sheikh killed about ninety people.

Europe, too, has been the target of Islamic suicide attacks. In March 2004, another group affiliated with al Qaeda claimed responsibility for bomb attacks on commuter trains in Madrid, Spain, that killed nearly two hundred people and left more than eighteen hundred injured. Many officials, too, believe that al Qaeda was behind the July 2005 suicide bombings of mass transit trains in London that killed fifty-two people.

A Global Security Threat

Today, although certain volatile regions (such as Israel, Iraq, and Chechnya) experience most of the world's terrorist strikes, virtually no country is immune from the possibility of suicide attacks. As Dr. Andrew

Silke, a London forensic psychologist and terrorism expert, summarizes, "In the past 20 years, 17 groups in 14 different countries have used suicide tactics. . . . They have killed more than 5,000 people, maimed at least 20,000 more and inflicted economic damage estimated at more than . . . [$122 billion]."[8]

At the same time, the risk of being harmed in a suicide terror attack for most people is very slim. As American doctors Robert L. DuPont, Elizabeth DuPont Spencer, and Caroline M. DuPont point out, "The odds of being killed by terrorists are very small compared to everyday risks such as death from smoking or car accidents."[9] De-

spite these low odds, suicide terrorism provokes a great deal of fear and anxiety because people have virtually no control over when or if a suicide bomber might strike, and if an attack occurs, the consequences can be immediate and catastrophic.

Despite the relatively low risk for individual citizens, governments perceive suicide terror as a clear threat. Random suicide terrorism is difficult to predict, prevent, or defend against; each bomb can cause great human, economic, and psychological damage. In countries where the tactic is part of a civil war or independence struggle, a systematic campaign of suicide terror can demoralize government troops and disrupt

Madrid is rocked by terrorist bomb attacks on commuter trains. Nearly two hundred people died; a thousand people were injured.

efforts to settle differences with negotiations. For the United States, the current spate of Islamic suicide bombings threatens to undermine citizens' support for U.S. foreign policies and weaken alliances with other nations. The bombings seem to express a worldwide wave of Muslim hostility toward America that can be very damaging to American economic and other interests. The specter of angry terrorists acquiring weapons of mass destruction further increases the danger. For these and other reasons, suicide terror is now one of the most challenging problems facing the world's leaders.

Chapter Two

What Motivates Suicide Bombers?

Terrorism experts have examined many different motivations for suicide terrorism, including psychological factors, poverty, religion, and political grievances. Many experts say there is no longer a typical profile for individual suicide bombers. Most suicide bombers, however, do not act alone; they are usually affiliated with an organization or group that uses suicide terrorism as a tactic to achieve a particular goal. Understanding these terrorist groups, experts say, is the key to fighting suicide terror.

The Profile of a Suicide Bomber

The typical profile of a suicide bomber perpetuated by politicians and the media is that of a poor, uneducated, and mentally unstable or criminal young male—a cowardly loner who has been brainwashed by a terrorist organization into becoming a suicide terrorist. Yet experts who have studied suicide terrorism say this profile is incorrect. Instead, suicide bombers tend to be young adults, either male or female, well educated and living a comfortable life, surrounded by family and friends. Some have children. Most have no criminal or terrorist past. They typically volunteer to become suicide bombers and their families are often the last to know about their suicide pact. As University of Michigan anthropologist and psychologist Scott Atran explains, "Suicide terrorists often are labeled crazed cowards bent on senseless destruction who thrive in the midst of poverty and ignorance. . . . What research there is, however, indicates that suicide terrorists have no appreciable psychopathology and are at least as educated

A young Iraqi Kurd, wired for a suicide bombing, was apprehended before he could complete his mission.

people. According to Terry McDermott, author of a book about the September 11 bombers called *Perfect Soldiers,* the men were from comfortable families and most had been educated in the West or were familiar with Western culture. Muhammad Atta, the hijacker who piloted the first plane to hit the World Trade Center, was a serious, pious thirty-three-year-old from a middle-class family in Egypt who had done graduate work in architecture in Germany. Marwan al-Shehhi, who piloted the second plane into the Trade Center, was a twenty-three-year-old member of the United Arab Emirates army and was described by McDermott as an "easygoing, robust, hail-fellow-well-met young man who loved to sing and laugh."[11] Hani Hanjour, the hijacker who crashed a third plane into the Pentagon, was reportedly a quiet, friendly, polite twenty-nine-year-old Saudi who spent a lot of time surfing the Internet. Ziad al-Jarrah, the hijacker of the fourth plane, which crashed in Pennsylvania, was twenty-six years old, happily married, and grew up in an easygoing, secular, middle-class Lebanese family that seemed to enjoy Western culture. Despite their apparent ordinariness, however, all these men

and economically well off as their surrounding populations."[10]

Fifteen of the nineteen al Qaeda hijackers responsible for the September 11 attacks, for example, were quite ordinary chose to take part in an attack that killed thousands of innocent people.

Nor is the modern suicide bomber always male. Although some Islamic terrorist groups such as al Qaeda have been reluctant to use women for suicide bombings, women increasingly have undertaken suicide missions on behalf of Sri Lankan, Palestinian, and Chechen causes. In 1985, nineteen-year-old Loula Abboud, an educated, middle-class Christian Lebanese woman, pioneered the phenomenon of women suicide bombers

A Hamas Terrorist Speaks

As part of her research, Harvard professor and terrorism expert Jessica Stern interviewed twenty-eight-year-old Hassan Salameh, a senior operative of Hamas, a Palestinian group known for its suicide bomb attacks on Israel. Salameh was arrested and jailed by Israel for organizing a suicide bombing campaign in 1996 that killed more than sixty people. Salameh justifies suicide bombings against Israelis this way: "As a Palestinian, I feel that my people and I have been murdered in the soul by the Israeli occupation. . . . There is a big difference between murder and killing to defend [my] country—attacks against Israelis, even against Israeli citizens, are the latter kind of killing, not murder. All religions allow people the right to kill in self-defense, or to defend their land. Land has been taken from us with violence, and we have the right to take it back."

Quoted in Jessica Stern, *Terror in the Name of God.* New York: HarperCollins, 2003, p. 59.

Palestinian terrorist group Hamas founder Sheikh Ahmed Yassin gives an interview in the Gaza Strip in 2001.

and became an instant Lebanese and Palestinian heroine when she blew herself up in front of a group of Israeli soldiers in Lebanon. In 1991, it was a female Tamil Tiger who assassinated former Indian prime minister Rajiv Gandhi. In 2002, twenty-eight-year-old Wafa Idriss conducted the first female Palestinian suicide bomb attack inside Israel when she walked into a shopping district in Jerusalem and blew up herself and an eighty-one-year-old Israeli man. Since 2000, most of the Chechen suicide bombers, too, have been female. Today, even some al Qaeda–affiliated terrorists have been women, as evidenced by reports of female bombers in Iraq.

With this range of age, background, and sex characteristics, it is almost impossible to predict who might become a suicide bomber today. As an officer in the Israel Defense Forces explains, "There is no clear profile anymore—not for terrorists and especially not for suicide bombers."[12]

Psychological Factors

Research has clearly shown that suicide bombers do not tend to be depressed or suicidal or suffer from mental illness. Ariel Merari, a psychologist at Tel Aviv University in Israel and a respected expert on Middle Eastern terrorism, has researched the background of every suicide bomber in the Middle East since 1983 and has concluded, "In the majority [of suicide terrorists] you find none of the risk factors normally associated with suicide, such as mood disorders or schizophrenia, substance abuse or history of attempted suicides."[13]

Instead of depression, most experts say, suicide bombers are motivated by strong feelings of hatred, humiliation, alienation, and despair caused by real or perceived social or political grievances. American clinical psychologist Rona Fields, who has researched terrorism in eleven countries, explains, "The main thing is that terrorism is a choice people make. . . . It's not a sickness. . . . It's a choice they make when they feel that their group is threatened. It's a level of retributive justice; it's vendetta, not psychosis."[14]

For Palestinian terrorists, for example, much of the suicide terror against Israel is simply retaliatory—vengeance for what are seen as brutal and excessive Israeli military actions against Palestinians and occupation of Palestinian lands. As Mia Bloom, a political scientist at the University of Cincinnati, explains, "Suicide bombing is an effort to punish and deter Israeli actions and to create a 'balance of terror.' The Palestinians seek to persuade Israelis that they will pay a high price for the occupation and force them to pressure their government to withdraw from the Territories and thus end the occupation."[15] For some Islamic terrorists, the reasons for retribution are even more amorphous—globalization, the spread of Western power, and hatred and resentment of superpower America in general.

The Effects of Poverty and Education

Nor does poverty or lack of education seem to be a major root cause of suicide terror-

Contrary to the popular image of terrorists as poor and uneducated, these Hamas suicide bombers most likely hold college degrees and come from middle-class families.

ism. Alberto Albadie, an associate professor for public policy at Harvard, example, studied the link between overall terrorism and economic status and found that the risk of terrorism is not significantly higher for poor countries than for rich ones. As Albadie told the *Harvard Gazette*, "In the past, we heard people refer to the strong link between terrorism and poverty, but in fact when you look at the data, it's not there."[16] Instead, Albadie found that the level of political freedom is a stronger indicator of terrorism than poverty. Ironically, those countries with an intermediate level of political openness experience the most terrorism. Under very autocratic regimes, such as Iraq under Saddam Hussein, citizens are likely to avoid any type of act that could be viewed as political because they fear that they or their families will be punished with prison, torture, or death. In countries with broad political freedoms, such as the United States, a very liberal right to dissent appears to discourage terrorism.

Studies of individual suicide bombers from many different terrorist groups have likewise demonstrated little connection between terrorism and either poverty or education. Unlike common criminals, who often tend to have low incomes and education levels, suicide bombers do not tend to be poor or uneducated. Researchers Basel Saleh and Claude Berrebi, for example, found that the majority of Palestinian suicide bombers had a college education (as compared to only 15 percent of the population of the same age) and that less than 15 percent were from poor families. Similarly, Princeton economist Alan B. Krueger and Czech professor Jitka Maleckova claim that suicide bombers from groups such as Hiz-ballah and Hamas are "more likely to come from economically advantaged families and have a relatively high degree of education as to come from the ranks of the economically disadvantaged and uneducated."[17] A number of the al Qaeda detainees held by the United States at Guantánamo, Cuba, reportedly have graduate degrees and come from high-status families. The same pattern is true for the leaders of organizations that employ suicide bombers. Most of Hamas's top leadership is highly educated, and Osama bin Laden, the leader of al Qaeda, is widely known to be a man of great wealth and education.

Krueger and Maleckova explain that terrorism is really "a violent form of political engagement" and that "more educated people from privileged backgrounds are more likely to participate in politics . . . because political involvement requires some minimum level of interest, expertise, and commitment to issues . . . all of which are more likely if people have enough education and income to concern themselves

A leader of the Tamil Tigers speaks in Sri Lanka. Some terrorist leaders are paid well for their services.

with more than minimum economic subsistence."[18] Indeed, researchers say that educated, prosperous candidates may actually be sought out as recruits by terrorist groups precisely because they are more dedicated to the cause, more inclined to be successful in the mission, and better able to fit into society in the places targeted by suicide bombers.

Most terrorism experts, however, agree that sometimes there is a correlation between support for suicide terrorism and economic factors. During a period of economic stagnation, such as has existed in Palestinian areas for decades, financial incentives from terrorist groups help to ensure both a ready pool of volunteers and acceptance of the terrorist group by society as a whole. In addition to salaries, terrorist groups often provide much-needed social assistance, in the form of schooling, food, and jobs, to the community. Also, families of dead suicide bombers are sometimes given relatively large monetary rewards, so the bombers know that their death will at least help their family to survive. In poor cultures with few other opportunities to rise above poverty, this material aid can be a strong motivation. As Israeli sociology professor Baruch Kimmerling explains, "When a starving refugee family has ten or twelve kids with no prospects for a proper education, stable employment or suitable marriages, the appeal to 'donate' one or two children to Allah becomes very seductive. In exchange, the family receives considerable 'charity' funds, honor and social recognition."[19]

In these cases, U.S. terrorism expert Jessica Stern says, "such a person makes a cost-benefit analysis about the value of his life versus the value of his death, [and] he attaches greater value to death—both for his country and for himself."[20] Stern criticizes terrorist groups for actively preying upon the poor and the ignorant. Some Middle East groups, she claims, fund seminaries or orphanages for the poor, and then recruit young men from these institutions into their terrorist operations. As Stern explains, "These foot soldiers often function as cannon fodder, with minimal training."[21]

Cash Bonuses

Terrorist organizations also pay their leaders, managers, and trainers quite well, causing some observers to wonder whether their motivation for terrorism is at least partly economic. These leadership positions can also be very attractive because leaders are not required to blow themselves up. One militant trainer who teaches foreign languages for a Middle Eastern terrorist group, for example, reported being paid more than twice the amount he made working as a teacher before he joined the organization. Groups also offer cash bonuses to managers for their success in areas such as recruiting and conducting terrorist operations. Some militants have become disillusioned with their organizations because of this emphasis on financial rewards. One Pakistani militant, for example, told Stern, "Initially I was of the view that [the organization's leaders] are doing

The Story of an Iraqi Suicide Terrorist

In an interview with Time *magazine in 2005, an operative who facilitates Iraqi suicide bombings explained his duties and motivations. The man, who used the pseudonym Abu Qaqa al-Tamimi, was once a member of Iraq's elite military, the Republican Guard, but now acts as a handler for those who volunteer to become suicide bombers for the insurgency. He hides suicide volunteers in safe houses, feeds them, trains them, helps them to choose targets, and provides them with explosives. Al-Tamimi explains:*

"My job is to know how I can get a bomber to the best spot for an attack, at a time when he is sure to inflict the most damage." Since September 2004, al-Tamimi claims to have helped coordinate at least thirty suicide bombings, both for Sunni insurgent groups and for al-Zarqawi's al Qaeda fighters. One of these was an attempted assassination of an Iraqi general in Fallujah in June 2005 that resulted in the deaths of three Iraqi soldiers and two civilians.

Quoted in Aparisim Ghosh, "Professor of Death: An Iraqi Insurgent Leader Reveals How He Trains and Equips Suicide Bombers and Sends Them on Their Lethal Missions," *Time*, October 24, 2005, p. 44.

Abu Musab al-Zarqawi led the Iraqi insurgency sponsored by al Qaeda. He was killed by U.S. forces on June 7, 2006.

jihad [holy war], but now I believe that it is a business and people are earning wealth through it. . . . The real thing is that it is a business empire."[22]

The Role of Religion

Because so many of the suicide bombings that have taken place around the world in recent years have been carried out by Islamic fundamentalists, many scholars suggest that religion is playing an increasingly important part in today's suicide attacks. As Scott Atran, research director at the National Center for Scientific Research in Paris, explains: "Suicide attacks were perhaps once mainly organized campaigns aimed at ending perceived occupation of the attackers' homeland. . . . But [they] are now mostly religiously motivated actions by small, loosely connected groups to exorcise cultural humiliation, of which military occupation may be just one manifestation."[23]

American terrorism expert Jessica Stern agrees that religion is a factor in modern suicide attacks, noting, "If you look at the number of fatalities, it's very clear Islamist groups are most lethal."[24] Stern, who spent four years interviewing religious terrorists around the world, says religion often is the key that transforms ordinary people into spiritually intoxicated suicide killers:

My interviews suggest that people join religious terrorist groups partly to transform themselves and to simplify life. They start out feeling humiliated, enraged that they are viewed by some Other as second class. They take on new identities as martyrs on behalf of a purported spiritual cause. . . . The weak become strong. The selfish become altruists, ready to make the ultimate sacrifice of their lives in the belief that their deaths will serve the public good. Rage turns to conviction. What seems to happen is that they enter a kind of trance, where the world is divided neatly between good and evil, victim and oppressor. Uncertainty and ambivalence, always painful to experience, are banished.[25]

Some terrorism experts, in fact, see Islamic fanaticism as the key to modern suicide terror. According to psychiatrist and terrorism researcher Marc Sageman, many Muslims have become disillusioned with the decline of Islamic culture and the inability of Arabs to advance their civilizations in the modern world. For a growing number of Muslims, the answer to this problem is the reestablishment of a fundamentalist version of Islam and the creation of Islamic governments that will strictly enforce core, conservative Islamic values. Some Muslims advocate peaceful means to achieve these goals, but the creation and spread of al Qaeda in recent years has galvanized a new, more militant movement. These militant Muslims are willing to use violence, including suicide terrorism, characterizing it as a holy war, or jihad, justified by their religious ends. As Sageman explains, "The global [Islamic] jihad is a worldwide revivalist movement with the goal of reestablishing past Muslim glory in a great Islamist state stretching from Morocco to the Philippines."[26]

Whether or not religion is their key motivator, today's fundamentalist Islamic terrorist groups, such as Hamas and al Qaeda, clearly wrap themselves in religious rhetoric and interpret the Koran, Islam's sacred book, in ways that fit their objectives. They urge Muslims to join them as part of an Islamic war against Western infidels and promise that suicide bombers will be viewed as Islamic martyrs and given spiritual rewards. Religiously oriented groups, some say, may be the most dangerous because they seem to be able to attract a larger pool of suicide volunteers than more secular groups. As scholar Mia Bloom explains,

> Religious ideology or political culture can be crucial . . . [and can] inspire a

U.S. troops raid a compound in Kandahar in southern Afghanistan. American forces continually search for terrorist hiding places.

self-perpetuating subculture of martyrdom. Children who grow up in such settings may be subtly indoctrinated into a culture glorifying ultimate sacrifice in the service of the cause.... Palestinian children as young as six report that they want to grow up and become [martyrs].... By the age of twelve they are fully committed and appreciate what becoming a martyr entails.[27]

Terrorist Organizations and Political Goals

Regardless of the motivations, experts in the terrorism field agree that most suicide terror is perpetrated not by individuals but by terrorist organizations that recruit individuals to carry out attacks. The typical suicide bomber today is connected to an organization that has conducted reconnaissance, built the explosive device, identified the target, and given instructions for detonation. The bomber has been psychologically prepared by the organization and delivered by a handler as close to the target as possible. In some cases, the bomb is even detonated by remote control, giving the organization even more control over the operation. As Boaz Ganor, head of the International Policy Institute for Counter-Terrorism in Israel, explains, "If one wants to understand the phenomenon [of terrorism], do not understand the motivation of the perpetrator but the motivation of the organization."[28]

Most of these terrorist organizations, experts agree, have decidedly political goals—that is, they have a real or perceived grievance against a particular enemy and they seek specific remedies that often involve changes in political policies. One of the most vocal proponents of this view is University of Chicago political scientist Robert Pape, who conducted extensive research on suicide bombers for his 2005 book, *Dying to Win: The Strategic Logic of Suicide Terrorism*. He concludes that most modern suicide terrorists are nationalist insurgents with a nonreligious, strategic goal—ousting military troops from the occupation of what they view as their land or territory. In most cases, the troops are those of democratic governments, which terrorists see as more vulnerable to terrorist pressure than highly authoritarian regimes. As Pape explains, "Suicide-terrorist attacks are ... driven by... a clear strategic objective: to compel modern democracies to withdraw military forces from the territory that the terrorists view as their homeland.... Every major suicide-terrorist campaign—over 95 percent of all the incidents—has had as its central objective to compel a democratic state to withdraw."[29]

This pattern, Pape claims, can be seen in Lebanon, the Palestinian-Israeli conflict, Sri Lanka, and Chechnya. Hizballah fought to oust Israel from Lebanon, just as Palestinian terrorist groups now demand that Israel withdraw from lands claimed by Palestinians. Sri Lanka and Chechnya also both fight for nationalist causes, demanding independence of their people and lands from what they view as oppressive governments. Another example is Osama bin Laden, who began his war against the United States by railing against the presence of American combat forces in Saudi Arabia (even though they were there with the consent of the Saudi government). Bin Laden predicted that the United States had a grand plan to conquer Iraq and Saudi Arabia in order to give land to Israel. The subsequent U.S. invasion of Iraq seemed to fulfill this prediction, helping bin Laden mobilize large numbers of volunteer fighters in Iraq, many of them from Saudi Arabia.

Today, the number of U.S. forces in Arab countries has increased to about 150,000, most of them in Iraq, and Iraq is now the undisputed center for suicide terrorism. As Pape explains, "Before our invasion, Iraq never had a suicide-terrorist attack in its history. Never. Since our invasion, suicide terrorism has been escalating rapidly with 20 attacks in 2003, 48 in 2004, and over 50 in just the first few months of 2005. Every year that the United States has stationed 150,000 combat troops in Iraq, suicide terrorism has doubled."[30]

Pape argues that once occupying forces withdraw from the homeland territory of the terrorists, the terrorism often abruptly stops. He points to Lebanon, which had forty-one suicide attacks between 1982 and 1986, but almost none after U.S., French, Italian, and Israeli forces withdrew from most of the Lebanese territory. Another example, Pape says, is the Israeli-Palestinian conflict, where there has been a major decline in suicide terrorism since Israel began withdrawing from Gaza, one of the territories claimed by Palestinians. As Pape explains, "Withdrawal of military forces really does diminish the ability of the terrorist leaders to recruit more suicide terrorists."[31]

According to this analysis, religion may be a motivator or an aid to attracting recruits. It may also be used to demonize the enemy. In most cases, however, terrorist groups undertake suicide missions to achieve clear political goals.

Chapter Three

How Is Suicide Terrorism Justified?

Even assuming that the goals or motivations of suicide bombers, or the groups recruiting them, have merit as struggles against injustice or foreign occupation, most people take the position that suicide bombings can never be justified on moral grounds. However, suicide terror is a form of unconventional warfare that makes sense from a military standpoint, and it is sometimes effective, making it a very attractive option for terrorist groups.

The Morality of Suicide Bombing

Many people around the world view any type of terrorist strike, particularly suicide terror, as an immoral act, especially if it targets civilians. Most religions, for example, view suicide bomb attacks as a sin. Despite the growing numbers of fundamentalist

Islamic terrorists, most Muslims believe that Islam forbids both murder and suicide. Some Islamic clerics have even issued fatwas, or religious edicts, against suicide bombing. On July 14, 2005, for example, Britain's largest Sunni Muslim organization, the Sunni Council, issued a binding religious fatwa condemning the suicide attacks that killed dozens of people on London subway trains and a double-decker bus on July 7. The group's chair, Mufti Muhammad Gul Rehman Qadri, called the bombings anti-Islamic, explaining, "Who has given anyone the right to kill others? . . . What happened in London can be seen as a sacrilege. It is a sin to take your life or the life of others."[32] The Sunni Council also specifically denounced Muslims who use events in Israel and Iraq to justify their suicide attacks.

The conscious targeting of civilians seems to provoke the most widespread condemnation. For example, Saudi Arabia's highest-ranking religious leader, Sheikh Abd al-Aziz bin Abdallah al-Sheikh, spoke out against al Qaeda's suicide tactics in the 1998 attacks against U.S. embassies in Kenya and Tanzania: "Any explosion that leads to the death of innocent women and children is a criminal act, carried out only by people who are base cowards and traitors. A rational person with only a small portion of respect and virtue refrains from such operations."[33] Similarly, al Qaeda's 9/11 attack in the United States sparked outrage around the world, including among Muslims, largely because so many innocent civilians were deliberately killed.

For some Muslims, however, suicide tactics are morally abhorrent only under certain circumstances. Extremist groups that use suicide tactics against an occupying army or its government officials are sometimes viewed sympathetically as "freedom fighters" engaged in a legitimate war, even if civilians are harmed in the process. Some very mainstream Muslim religious leaders, for example, see suicide bombings as justified if the purpose is to repel an occupying force. As Sayed Muhammad Musawi, head of the World Islamic League in London, has stated, "There should be a

The twisted wreckage of this double-decker bus is all that remains after the London bombings of July 7, 2005.

clear distinction between the suicide bombing of those who are trying to defend themselves from occupiers, . . . [and the bombing of] civilians, which is a big crime."[34] What constitutes an occupier, however, is subject to many different interpretations. When the bombers target civilians as well as soldiers, the question becomes even murkier. Among the Muslim community, for example, there are wide differences about whether the suicide bombings in Iraq, Chechnya, and Israel are permitted by the Koran. For those who try to justify suicide terror as a reasonable response to foreign occupation or other injustice, the task of establishing a bright line of morality is a difficult one.

The Cult of Martyrdom for a Higher Cause

More radical followers of Islam go a step further to justify their suicide terror. They claim that suicide missions are an act of martyrdom, a holy sacrifice endorsed by Islam in circumstances where an injustice is unbearable. In 2004, for example, the executioners of Nick Berg, an American contractor in Iraq, referred to a Koran passage (5:32–35) that states, "Whoever kills a human being, except as punishment for murder or other villainy in the land, shall be regarded as having killed all mankind." Islamic extremists interpret the middle part of this verse as a loophole to mean that the Koran permits killing if it is a response to "murder and villainy." For these radical Islamists, the West has committed such "villainy" by invading Muslim lands and spread-

ing Western values that violate the radical Muslims' understanding of Islamic law.

Similarly, many Palestinians justify suicide bombing of Israeli civilians as a result of the despair created by Israel's occupation of Palestinian lands. As Eyad Sarraj, a Palestinian psychiatrist and founder of the Palestinian Independent Commission for Citizens' Rights, explains: "Ours is a nation of anger and defiance. The struggle today is how not to become a suicide bomber. . . . What propels people into such action is a long history of humiliation and a desire for revenge that every Arab harbors. . . . For the extremist militant, there is no difference between Israelis. They are the enemy; they are all the same."[35]

Some Palestinian supporters even claim that what is truly immoral is the public's focus on the violence of the suicide bombers because it pales in comparison to the violence done by the Israeli army against the Palestinian people. As human rights advocate Chandra Muzaffar puts it,

> It is a travesty of justice to blame suicide bombers for the Israeli-Palestinian conflict. For we are talking of young men and women from a community which has been dispossessed, disinherited and disenfranchised. We are talking of a people who have been driven out from their land by Israeli aggression and occupation—a land which they had tilled and toiled upon for thousands of years. Deprived of hearth and home, denied rights and

An Islamic extremist group claimed it killed American Nick Berg (seated) as revenge for U.S. actions in Iraq.

liberties, the Palestinians are struggling against formidable odds to preserve what little is left of their honour and their dignity.... How can one compare the violence perpetrated by one of the most well-equipped armies in the world with the violence of a largely unarmed, defenceless people relying upon a small [cache] of smuggled weapons?[36]

This argument essentially holds that suicide tactics are morally justifiable because the cause is righteous—in other words, the ends justify the means. Indeed, terror-

ists typically see the world in very black and white terms and their movement as such an epic struggle of good against evil that extremism becomes acceptable. As Jessica Stern explains, "Because [terrorists] believe their cause is just, and because the population they hope to protect is purportedly so deprived, abused, and helpless, they persuade themselves that any action—even a heinous crime—is justified. They know they are right, not just politically, but morally. They believe God is on their side."[37]

Some of the incentives used to recruit suicide bombers further justify the terrorists' cause. Radical Muslim leaders, for example, promise that potential suicide recruits will have a glorious death and be rewarded by Allah with Paradise. Martyrs even achieve a type of superstardom; they are seen as heroes who have made the ultimate sacrifice for their people, an act that assures them and their families of high status and great honor in their community. Indeed, so many Palestinian youths are vying to become suicide bombers today that Hamas must turn many away. As a Hamas operative has stated, "The selection process is complicated by so many people wanting to be taken on this journey of honor! If we choose one, countless others are disappointed. They have to learn to be patient and to wait until God calls them!"[38]

Many Muslims reject an interpretation of Islam that justifies the killing of innocents under any circumstances. Irshad Manji, a Canadian author and critic of fundamentalist Islam, urges Muslims to acknowledge that the Koran, like the Bible, contains both peaceful and vengeful scriptures. Manji believes that selected passages have been inappropriately used by fundamentalists to fuel today's rash of terrorist activity.

The Military Logic of Suicide Bombing

Whether or not terrorist organizations find justification in religious texts, analysts say that most of those who use suicide tactics do so for purely practical reasons. As Ayatollah Sayyid Muhammad Husayn Fadlallah, the most senior Shiite cleric affiliated with Hizballah, has explained, "[A suicide mission] differs little from that of a soldier who fights and knows that in the end he will be killed. The two situations lead to

Vigilante Justice

Although Palestinian suicide bombers find many ways to justify the killing of civilians, one expert says their actions are little more than vigilante justice. Dr. Ben Saul, a law professor at the University of New South Wales, rejects the argument often made by Palestinian extremists that Israeli settlers are not innocent noncombatants, but rather knowing instruments of Israel's illegal policy of occupying Palestinian lands. Although the killing of civilians can be justified under international law, in cases in which the civilians work in munitions factories or are otherwise militarily dangerous to an adversary, Saul argues that the killing of Israeli settlers, or the killing of Israelis living inside Israel, is unlawful, even as a reprisal for Israeli acts, because such civilians pose no military danger. The killing of such civilians, he says, is nothing more than vigilante justice and vengeance.

death; except that one fits in with the conventional procedures of war, and the other does not. . . . There is no difference between dying with a gun in your hand or exploding yourself."[39]

Suicide bombings, in fact, are a very useful unconventional war tactic against countries or governments with often formidable armies and equipment, in situations where more conventional warfare would either be unsuccessful or produce too many casualties. Instead of engaging a large army on the battlefield, where they would surely lose, terrorist groups use suicide bombings as a way to level the playing field. As Sheikh Ahmed Yassin, the founder of Hamas, once explained, "Once we have warplanes and missiles, then we can think of changing our means of legitimate self-defense. But right now, we can only tackle the fire with our bare hands and sacrifice ourselves."[40]

Suicide bombs are also popular weapons because they are cheap, and most terrorist groups are small organizations with limited budgets. Indeed, suicide bombs

Prominently displayed posters of a Palestinian suicide bomber who succeeded in his mission show him as a hero, a martyr to the cause of Islam.

have been called the ultimate strategic weapon of the poor and the weak because they can inflict high casualties at a very low cost. Compared to conventional weapons and armies, which can cost billions, a suicide bombing requires only a willing volunteer, a bit of training and planning, and a few inexpensive bomb parts. Even the dramatic and complicated September 11 attack, according to federal experts, required only about $500,000 to pay for flight training, airline tickets, and the terrorists' living expenses as they prepared for attack.

Moreover, suicide bombers are very difficult to catch before they strike, and since they are already expecting to die, no type of force can deter them even if they are detected. Nor is any after-the-fact retaliation possible except for indirect actions against the bombers' families, their communities, or the groups that employ them. In addition, unlike many military missions, suicide bombings do not require an exit plan—that is, a way for the bomber to escape from the scene of the bombing. This is usually the most difficult part of any military operation. Because the suicide tactic is so hard to defend against, it can be used over and over, as long as there is a pool of willing volunteers.

Above all else, however, the suicide tactic is highly effective at instilling society-wide fear and terror that, the terrorists hope, will eventually weaken the will of the enemy and the public's support for its military missions in the targeted region. Terrorizing the population sends a message that no one will be safe until a particular policy of the offending government is changed. As an intelligence Web site called The Estimate explains, "Suicide bombing has an impact because it strikes directly at the heart of civilian society: the bomber could be almost anyone on the street, and if one target appears too secure, the bomber can simply select another."[41] The media become an unwitting accomplice in this terror strategy, because television crews and journalists flock to cover the dramatic aftermath of bombings, thereby spreading the terrorists' message of fear.

The Success of Suicide Terror

Terrorism experts say that suicide bombing is popular among terrorist organizations because it has sometimes been successful in achieving political and strategic objectives. In Lebanon, for example, most analysts credit Hizballah's suicide attacks with forcing the withdrawal of all U.S., French, and Italian troops from Lebanon in early 1984. Israel, which had gained Lebanese territory during its invasion of Lebanon in 1982, was also unable to cope with the prospect of unrelenting Hizballah attacks. Israel therefore abandoned much of that territory by June 1985 and completely retreated from all of Lebanon in May 2000. These successes, in turn, paved the way for Hizballah to participate in elections and become a mainstream political party that no longer needs to rely upon suicide bombings. Although still armed and hostile to Israel, Hizballah today controls most of southern Lebanon

A shopkeeper in Bethlehem sits amid the burned-out ruins of his store in 2002, another result of a widespread campaign of terror by Hizballah.

and is viewed by many Lebanese citizens as a heroic resistance force that defended the country against what was seen as Israeli aggression.

Suicide bombings also seem to have helped achieve the aims of Palestinian extremist groups such as Hamas, which has opposed the negotiating positions taken by the more moderate Palestine Liberation Organization (PLO) in its efforts to forge a peace agreement to end the Palestinian/Israeli conflict. Hamas bombings, for example, have been credited with derailing the 1995 Oslo Interim Agreement, an American-sponsored plan negotiated between Israel and the PLO that was sup-

posed to provide a process for future talks toward a final peace settlement.

Hamas attacks on Israel, however, have dwindled in recent years, reducing the level of fear among Israelis and creating an economic boom in Israel. Many Israelis claim that the decline of Hamas-inspired violence is due to their military success and the building of a defensive wall to stop Palestinians from traveling into Israeli settlements. Other observers, however, credit a conscious decision by Hamas to refrain from violence in order not to spoil Israel's decision to unilaterally withdraw from Gaza, one of the occupied territories claimed by the Palestinians. Instead, Hamas turned to politics, winning a landslide victory in Palestinian parliamentary elections in January 2006—a victory that gives the group new power and places it in a position to control the Palestinian response in any future peace talks with Israel. Following the election, Hamas leaders proposed a long-term cease-fire in return for Israel's withdrawal to the borders it had before the 1967 Arab-Israeli war—a proposition that Israel is unlikely to accept but one that some experts believe could lead to concrete negotiations between the two sides.

Similarly, in Sri Lanka, the Tamil Tigers have largely abandoned suicide missions since signing an agreement with the government in February 2002 that called for a cease-fire and provided for limited self-rule for Tamil areas in Sri Lanka. Peace talks also began but ended in 2003 when the Tigers withdrew. Since then, the cease-fire has held, albeit with an increasing number of violations by both sides.

More recently, in Spain, al Qaeda's suicide attacks on civilians helped to force that nation out of the American-led coalition fighting in Iraq—one of the group's main goals. According to an al Qaeda planning document found by Norwegian intelligence, al Qaeda is focusing on strikes against America's allies in order to split the coalition forces fighting in Iraq. The document recommended that Spain should be hit first, just before the March 2004 elections, because "Spain could not withstand two, maximum three, blows before withdrawing from the coalition, and then others would fall like dominoes."[42] In fact,

this is exactly what happened. Al Qaeda suicide bombers set off explosives in Spain's commuter trains on the morning of March 11, 2004, killing 191 people and wounding 1,460. An antiwar party won the subsequent Spanish election and on April 17, 2004, Spain withdrew from the Iraq coalition, followed by numerous other countries, including Italy, Portugal, Moldova, the Philippines, Thailand, Honduras, New Zealand, and the Dominican Republic. In the view of many terrorism experts, the success of al Qaeda's suicide attacks has made the terrorist group stronger than ever before. Indeed, some experts think that the reason al Qaeda has not attacked inside the United States since September 11 is because it has focused on other targets.

Political observers point out, however, that suicide bombings can undercut a people's struggle for justice. Some analysts suggest, for example, that the Palestinians under Israeli occupation garnered much more sympathy among Israelis and around the world before they resorted to suicide bombings. During their first mass uprising, called the First Intifada, men, women, and children armed only with stones protested Israel's policies and faced down Israel's elite military—an unequal confrontation that resulted in widespread criticism of Israel. In recent years, during the period called the Second Intifada, militant Palestinian groups (such as Hamas) forfeited worldwide sympathy by their string of suicide bombings against Israeli soldiers and civilians. These bombings, critics say, destroyed Israel's growing peace movement,

Chechnya's "Black Widows"

The vast majority of Chechen suicide attacks have been carried out by women. These terrorists have been nicknamed "Black Widows" because many of them have lost husbands, fathers, brothers, and/or sons in the Chechen-Russian war. Many experts believe they are driven to suicide terrorism because of overwhelming rage, despair, and grief caused by the horrendous war in Chechnya and the many human rights abuses committed by Russian troops. The circumstances of many bombings seem to support this view. One typical suicide attack occurred in November 2001, for example, when Luiza Gazueva killed herself and a Russ-

ian military commandant who had killed her husband during an interrogation. On August 24, 2004, another suicide bomber, Aminat Nagaeva, blew up a small jet over southern Russia to avenge the killing of her brother by government troops. Days later, on September 2, Nagaeva's sister, Roza, was the bomber held responsible for a blast at the Moscow Rizhskaya Metro station, which killed ten people. Roza's son had been killed, along with her and Aminat's brother, by Russian forces. She bribed Russian soldiers to retrieve her son's body, which showed he had been severely beaten and tortured with electricity before his death.

A Chechen "Black Widow" speaks at her sentencing in a Moscow court. Most suicide bombers from Chechnya are female.

Medical personnel remove bodies from a bombed commuter train in Madrid in 2004. The terrorist strikes were designed to pressure Spain's withdrawal from Iraq.

provided the government a pretext to use massive military force to crush Palestinian communities, and helped bring about the election of a highly conservative Israeli leader, Prime Minister Ariel Sharon.

Alternative Strategies

Although suicide tactics sometimes achieve political goals, some observers believe that suicide bombings create a spiral of death that can never humble a committed occupying force or provide true hope to an oppressed people. A few activists advocate an alternate strategy of pacifism—a peace-ful, nonviolent means of resistance—as a better way to resist injustice. Muslim-American peace activist Ramzi Kysia, for example, argues that pacifism should be applied in the Israeli-Palestinian conflict because decades of violent struggle have been largely unsuccessful in bringing long-term peace or prosperity to the Palestinians. Instead of violence, Kysia says that "Palestinians must [simply] refuse to be occupied and resist with a righteousness that provokes love in their enemies. They must resist with life, not death. The uproar this will cause in Israel, and the massive, worldwide pressure it will put on Israel . . . will bring peace. The Israeli government can be overthrown—but only through a resistance that provokes the Israeli people to overthrow it for themselves."[43]

Kysia suggests many tactics that Palestinians could employ in a nonviolent struggle, such as ignoring curfews in occupied territories, publicly burning identity cards required by Israel, and peacefully marching through checkpoints and military zones that are closed to Palestinians, even if that provokes the Israeli army to open fire. When asked for their names, Kysia says, Palestinians could give the names of political prisoners in Israeli jails. Palestinians could also begin a massive campaign of "illegal" Palestinian home construction and land development in occupied lands. Many of these actions would lead to arrest, or even death, but Kysia argues that such courageous nonviolence would reveal Israel to be the true aggressor and would flood and thereby cripple Israeli prisons.

Supporters of pacifism point out that nonviolence has been successful on many occasions throughout history. In India, for example, Mohandas Gandhi organized hundreds of thousands of Indians to engage in nonviolent, passive resistance that eventually forced Britain to end its colonial rule in India. Martin Luther King's peaceful protests helped to achieve civil rights for African Americans. In eastern Europe and the Soviet Union, largely nonviolent "people power" helped to bring down a number of entrenched Communist regimes. Nonviolence also has been used with success in the Muslim world. The Islamic revolution that overthrew the shah of Iran in 1979, for example, was largely a peaceful confrontation between unarmed men and women and government troops. And it was a mass, nonviolent movement that ultimately brought down Indonesian dictator Suharto in 1998.

Nonviolence, however, can be a very long-term strategy because it involves changing the thinking of millions of people. Such proposals seem unlikely to win many converts among extremists already committed to suicide terrorism.

Chapter Four

The Costs of Suicide Terrorism

The threat of suicide bombs creates psychological effects on both individuals and societies as well as many challenges for governments as they try to protect their citizens from this danger. The problem is especially difficult for democratic societies, which provide easy targets because of their openness and accessibility. In the United States, the September 11 suicide strike resulted in controversial, expensive, and ongoing conventional military actions abroad as well as skyrocketing costs for additional security and disaster readiness at home. Many citizens also fear that the wave of suicide terrorism and the government's attempt to combat it may be weakening many of the freedoms and privileges central to a democratic society. As journalist James Bovard comments, "The 9/11 attacks increased the [gullibility] of much of the American public. Politicians exploited that gullibility to seize more power, spend more money, and violate more rights."[44]

The Psychological Impact

Suicide terror typically creates a cycle of fear and trauma that ripples across the affected society. The people who pay the highest price in a suicide terror strike, of course, are those who die or are injured by the actual explosion. Many others directly exposed to the incident, such as first responders, bystanders who witness the death or injury of others, and the loved ones, family, and acquaintances of those killed, also experience a high degree of trauma, grief, and stress that may linger for months, years, and even lifetimes. Common symptoms include profound sadness or fear; distressing thoughts, feelings, or mental

First responders work their way through the rubble of the World Trade Center on September 11, 2001. The psychological toll of terrorism is profound.

images of the event; inability to sleep; frightening dreams; and problems with concentration.

The circle of trauma widens, however, to include many other people not directly affected by the incident. Children, especially those living near the area of the strike, for example, may become fearful that they or their families will become victims of a future attack. People with mental illnesses, those burdened with other recent losses or traumatic events, and individuals who are socially isolated often experience above-normal stress following a suicide attack. Workers in industries likely to be targeted by terrorists, such as those who work for the airlines or in government installations, also face a high risk of trauma. Indeed, even those who only experience the suicide terror episode vicariously, by watching television coverage, are affected. As the American Psychological Association notes, "Recent studies indicate that those who watched more television coverage of the terrorist attacks [on September 11, 2001] reported a higher degree of stress."[45]

How much people are traumatized by terrorism is determined largely by how often they are faced with terrorist violence. After 9/11, for example, most Americans recovered from the shock within six months. In Israel, however, which has been subjected

The 9/11 Commission's Report

The National Commission on Terrorist Attacks Upon the United States (commonly called the 9/11 Commission), created in 2002 to investigate the 9/11 terrorist attacks, found numerous government failures and recommended wide-ranging reforms. On December 5, 2005, the former commissioners, as part of the 9/11 Public Discourse Project, issued a bleak assessment of the government's antiterrorism efforts:

We are safer—no terrorist attacks have occurred within the United States since 9/11—but we are not as safe as we need to be. We see some positive changes. But there is so much more to be done. There are far too many C's, D's, and F's in the report card we will issue today. Many obvious steps that the American people assume have been completed, have not been. The leadership is distracted. Some of these failures are shocking. Four years after 9/11: It is scandalous that police and firefighters in large cities still cannot communicate reliably in a major crisis. It is scandalous that airline passengers are still not screened against all names on the terrorist watchlist. It is scandalous that we still allocate scarce homeland security dollars on the basis of pork barrel spending, not risk.

Remarks by Thomas H. Keen and Lee H. Hamilton, Final Report of the 9/11 Public Discourse Project, December 5, 2005. www.9-11pdp.org/press/2005-12-05_statement.pdf.

National Guard troops were brought in after 9/11 as added airline security.

to a barrage of suicide attacks over many years, people live in a state of continual danger and stress. In studies, many Israeli adults have reported experiencing some level of traumatic stress symptoms or depression, and children sometimes suffer even more from the ongoing state of fear. Every day brings a reminder of the threat. As reporter Flore de Préneuf explains,

In Israel, car trunks and handbags are systematically searched by security guards at the mall. People carrying large objects, wearing loose, baggy clothes or an Arab complexion are viewed suspiciously. . . . Most of all, living in a country plagued by terrorism means sacrificing a degree of personal liberty for a greater sense of security and constantly calculating the risks involved in carrying out ordinary activities such as driving, shopping and eating out. . . . Escapism, in particular, has become a dominant trait of Israeli society. People in Tel Aviv are famous for "partying on," no matter what. . . . Less flamboyantly, Israeli TV viewers have started to tune out the terror. Soap operas are up, news programs are down.[46]

omy. Economists say that suicide terror in Israel causes not only a loss of tourism dollars, but also a measurable decrease in consumer spending and a sizable drain on the national economy.

The Costs of Military Actions

The shock and fear created by suicide terrorism puts pressure on governments to take drastic actions to try to thwart this trend. Just days after the September 11 attack, for example, U.S. president George W. Bush declared a war on terrorism, promising to use every resource and tool to disrupt and defeat this new threat. Less than a month later, on October 7, 2001, the United States and Britain attacked Afghanistan's Taliban government, which they accused of harboring al Qaeda terrorists, and destroyed al Qaeda bases there. President Bush next targeted Iraq, which he claimed was sponsoring terrorism and seeking to develop chemical, biological, and nuclear weapons. On March 19, 2003, U.S. troops invaded Iraq and quickly overthrew the regime of Saddam Hussein, initiating a controversial war followed by a long, costly stabilization and reconstruction process.

Today, U.S. troops are still stationed in both countries, and they are expected to remain there for many more years to provide security while efforts are slowly made to rebuild the two governments and their societies. So far, more than twenty-five hundred American soldiers have died in Iraq, hundreds more have been killed in Afghanistan, and the monetary cost of

In addition, the feelings of fear and uncertainty created by suicide attacks, together with the limitation on mobility created by extra security, affect people's economic decisions and often have a negative effect on the economy of a region hit by such terrorism. Following the September 11 attack, for example, airline travel decreased significantly, causing dramatic economic losses for the airlines and many tourism industries that are dependent on air travel. These results were transitory, and the American public eventually returned to its normal pattern of air travel. In Israel, however, the ongoing threat of suicide attacks creates a steady burden on the econ-

An Iraqi citizen stomps on the toppled statue head of Saddam Hussein. U.S. troops removed Saddam from power after invading Iraq in 2003.

these ambitious operations has been astronomical. Since September 11, 2001, in fact, the United States has spent about $361 billion for military operations, reconstruction, and other programs in Iraq and Afghanistan, and it has plans to seek substantial additional funding for future activities in 2006 and beyond.

The military excursion into Iraq has also cost many Iraqi lives. The dangerous anti-American insurgency that has developed there collaborates with Islamic jihadists and conducts suicide attacks on both American soldiers and Iraqi civilians. Iraqis, in fact, are subjected to more sui-

cide attacks than any other society in the world. The U.S. Pentagon estimates that Iraqi insurgents have claimed twenty-six thousand Iraqi casualties (those both killed or wounded) since January 1, 2004. In 2005 alone, the Iraqi insurgency killed over forty-six hundred Iraqis. Although some of those attacks targeted elected leaders or soldiers, the vast majority of bomb victims were Iraqi civilians.

Also, despite the constant U.S. military efforts to root out the insurgents, the numbers of attacks and casualties are rising and insurgents are increasingly turning to suicide bombs as their weapon of choice. The number of bomb attacks—both suicide and traditional bomb attacks—increased from about thirty per day in October 2003 to one hundred per day in October 2005. Since April 2005, when Iraq's new government was formed, suicide attacks have mushroomed and now account for two out of every three insurgent bombings. In May 2005 alone, for example, a staggering ninety suicide attacks were conducted by Iraqi insurgents—almost as many as the total number of attacks Palestinian groups have carried out against Israel since 1993. The region now produces more suicide bombings than anywhere else on the globe.

The Costs of Security and Terror Preparedness

In addition to the costs of U.S. military engagements, the threat of suicide terror has resulted in escalating security and disaster readiness costs for Americans at home. After September 11, the U.S. government passed legislation that resulted in billions being spent on high-technology equipment designed to screen for weapons and bombs at airports, harbors, and federal sites. Under the 2001 Aviation and Transportation Security Act, all passenger baggage must be run through bomb and weapon screening machines or checked with handheld screeners. The machines required by the legislation cost roughly $1 million each to install, and because of their size and weight, the machines often required expensive reconfiguration of airports to accommodate them. The total cost of complying with the legislation nationwide has been estimated

at around $12 billion. Additional monies were spent to hire a new workforce of airport screeners, train armed air marshals to ride along on random flights, and secure federal buildings, seaports, and borders.

Added to these post–September 11 security expenditures are the costs for emergency preparedness to ensure that the country can adequately respond to future suicide terror strikes. To coordinate both security and emergency response in the wake of 9/11, the government created a huge new federal department, called Homeland Security, to oversee all domestic antiterrorist programs. The United States policymakers requested a budget of $41 billion for the Homeland Security Department, and experts say that the figure could easily double in a few years.

Despite the huge expenditures, many observers say that the new antiterror measures have only created an illusion that the government is keeping Americans safe. Former commissioners of the independent National Commission on Terrorist Attacks created to review the government failures behind the September 11 attacks, issued a report in December 2005, four years after the 9/11 tragedy. The commissioners found that Congress and the president had failed to enact adequate security and disaster readiness reforms. One of the commissioners' many criticisms was directed at the country's still inadequate cargo screening and border security. Today, for example, only a portion of all cargo reaching U.S. shores by air, boat, train, or truck is subject to inspection. Similarly, only about

5 percent of the tons of cargo and mail carried on commercial passenger aircraft within the United States is screened. Terrorists could easily plant a conventional explosive device, or even a biological or nuclear bomb, in a shipping crate or package and time it to go off once it reaches a U.S. port of entry or once a domestic passenger plane takes off.

Further criticism has been directed at the lack of protection for mass transit systems and dangerous sites such as chemical plants and nuclear power plants, which could be attacked by suicide terrorists with devastating results. The 9/11 commission also concluded that the nation was still lacking in other critical areas, such as creating a list of known terrorists that could

An airport security agent inspects the contents of a suitcase. Some new security measures are costly and time-consuming.

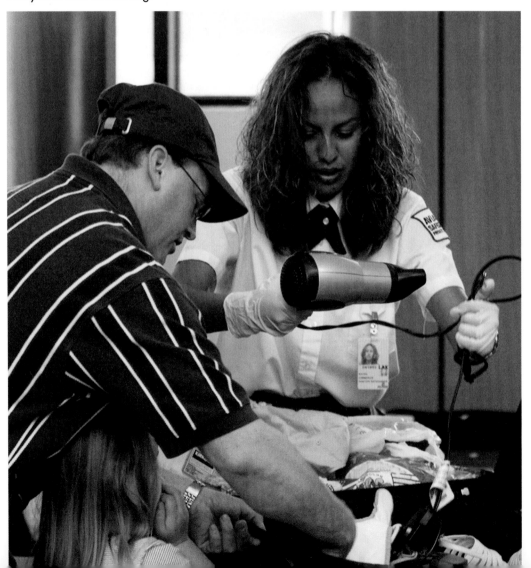

be used to alert airline officials about suspicious passengers, providing police and other emergency personnel with dedicated radio frequencies, and modern communications equipment. Additionally, cities would be awarded antiterrorism funds based on their risk of being hit with terrorist attacks. If improvements are made in these areas, they will undoubtedly result in even higher antiterrorism expenditures.

The government's inadequate response to a serious natural disaster—Hurricane Katrina—in 2005 clearly demonstrated further problems with the nation's emergency preparedness. The storm wiped out most of the city of New Orleans as well as coastal areas of Mississippi and Alabama. Yet many residents stranded in homes and shelters without food and water were not rescued for almost a week; housing and food aid was slow in coming; and six months later, thousands of storm victims still had no permanent place to live and little hope of putting their lives back together. If the government could not handle Katrina, a storm that was long predicted, people wondered how the country would handle a sudden, unpredicted terrorist attack in the middle of a large American city. As Ted Koppel, the former host of ABC's *Nightline* television program, reflected on August 30, 2005, "When you look at the damage inflicted by an accidental storm, you have to think about the sheer havoc that an intentional terrorist attack may produce one of these days."[47] Ironically, many people blamed a decision to make the Federal Emergency Management Agency

(FEMA), the federal agency that historically was charged with disaster preparedness, part of the new Homeland Security Department. This move, critics said, dismantled FEMA's proven emergency systems and eroded the country's disaster response expertise.

Altogether, including both military and domestic security costs, the U.S. war on terror is currently costing Americans about $7 billion each month, with $5.9 billion of that monthly outlay going to fund military operations in Iraq, according to the U.S. Congressional Budget Office. By 2010, experts say, the total cost of U.S. antiterror activities could escalate to at least $570 billion—more than half a trillion dollars. As U.S. Representative Peter King, a Republican from New York and a member of the House Homeland Security Committee, has explained, the war on terror is "a very expensive war."[48]

Reduced Democratic Freedoms

Perhaps the most dramatic consequence of the new trend of suicide terror, however, is not the money that is being spent for prevention and response. Some Americans worry more about how antiterrorism security measures are affecting individual freedoms and civil liberties—civil rights such as privacy and free speech, defining characteristics associated with American democracy. Many democratic, Western countries have faced this dilemma in recent years. Britain, for example, adapted its laws to allow British police to detain terrorism

Assessing the War in Iraq

Since its inception, the war in Iraq has been a controversial part of the U.S. struggle against terrorism. Although the administration of U.S. president George W. Bush has maintained that the war allows U.S. forces to fight terrorists abroad rather than inside the United States, many critics have questioned whether the Iraq operation is actually making U.S. citizens safe from terrorism. Poll results released in July 2005 revealed for the first time that nearly half of all Americans (47 percent) thought that the war in Iraq might actually damage the United States' ability to fight terrorism. Many of these citizens thought that the war had increased the chances of another terrorist attack inside the United States. The public also was increasingly critical of President Bush's handling of both the Iraq war and the overall fight to end terrorism. However, a narrow majority of respondents (52 percent) still believed that U.S. forces could stabilize Iraq and still supported keeping troops there until that goal is accomplished.

suspects for up to seven days without charges and deny them jury trials. The British public is also photographed by an estimated 1.5 million closed-circuit cameras positioned in public spaces to monitor for potential terrorist activities. Germany, after 9/11, enacted two controversial pieces of antiterror legislation that, among other things, increase regulation of private organizations and allow the prosecution in Germany of terrorist acts committed in foreign countries. In Israel, authorities routinely search bags for bombs at the entrances to shopping malls and other venues, and police are known to use certain forms of physical pressure in interrogations, such as painful handcuffing and sleep deprivation. Even Canada, known for its liberal views on civil liberties, allows police to hold terrorism suspects without bail for ninety days.

The United States, too, has responded to suicide terror with a vast expansion of police powers. Shortly after September 11, for example, President Bush proposed new legislation called the Patriot Act, which supporters said was necessary to provide law enforcement with new tools to crack down on terror. Congress passed the legislation with astonishing speed and little substantive review. The bill was introduced and passed in the House of Representatives on October 23 by a vote of 356 to 66, and it passed in the Senate without amendment two days later by a vote of 98 to 1. The act was signed into law on October 26, 2001.

The Patriot Act dramatically increased the right of the FBI and police to conduct searches of Americans' private property and records. Some of the most controversial sections of the new law concern personal information. Financial, library, travel, video rental, phone, medical, church, synagogue, and mosque records can be searched by law enforcement without people's knowledge or consent, and with only an administrative, instead of a judicial, subpoena. Other sections of the Patriot Act allow police to secretly search people's homes and property, tap their phones, and monitor their Internet communications, all without a warrant. The law also provides for a new crime called "domestic terrorism," which is defined as life-threatening acts against civilian populations in order to influence government policies or con-

duct. This category allows for the deportation of anyone who associates, even unknowingly, with terrorists and authorizes the temporary detention of aliens without any prior showing or court ruling that they are dangerous.

Although supporters of the law claim that the nation's law enforcement agencies need these extended powers to locate potential terrorists, many of these provisions of the Patriot Act have been criticized strongly by civil rights advocates as an assault on the individual freedoms that are vital in a democracy. According to the American Civil Liberties Union (ACLU), the

A demonstrator protests Patriot Act provisions that he believes are threats to free speech.

People at a Hamas terrorist camp burn the American flag in protest of American interference with and encroachment on the Muslim world.

legislation allows "law enforcement to conduct secret searches, gives them wide powers of phone and Internet surveillance, and access to highly personal medical, financial, mental health, and student records with minimal judicial oversight."[49] In addition, the ACLU says, the act allows FBI agents to investigate American citizens without probable cause and, in the name of "domestic terrorism," could subject political organizations to wiretapping, surveillance, and harassment based merely on their legal political activities. The Patriot Act's provisions, the ACLU argues, are an attack on Americans' personal privacy; threaten sacred constitutional rights such as freedom

of speech, freedom from unreasonable searches, and due process; and open the door to government abuses of power. Some law enforcement experts agree, arguing that the real problems that led to 9/11 were bureaucratic inefficiency, managerial incompetence, and restrictions on sharing intelligence information—problems that should be addressed by making law enforcement systems more accountable, not less.

Since the Patriot Act's passage, at least two federal courts have ruled parts of the law unconstitutional. In one decision, the court disapproved of a section of the act that made it a crime to give "expert advice or assistance" to groups designated as foreign terrorist organizations, finding it to be unconstitutionally vague. Another court struck down the provision in the act that allows for secret and unchallengeable searches of Internet and telephone records. The U.S. Justice Department is defending the legislation against these court challenges.

Many of the controversial provisions of the Patriot Act were set to expire at the end of 2005. President Bush and his supporters urged that the entire act be renewed, arguing that the federal government continues to need these expanded powers to protect America. Bush claimed that its provisions allowed the government to bring charges against more than four hundred suspects, more than half of whom have been convicted, and to break up terror cells and prosecute terrorist operatives and their supporters in a number of states. As the president put it, "The Patriot Act has accomplished exactly what it was designed to do—it has protected American liberty, and saved American lives."[50]

The Bush administration failed to win renewal in 2005, however, after news reports in December 2005 revealed that the president, even after the Patriot Act expanded law enforcement powers, secretly allowed another government agency to spy on Americans, possibly in violation of the law. Specifically, in 2002, President Bush authorized the National Se-

curity Agency (NSA)—a government intelligence agency charged with collecting information on foreigners—to spy on Americans and others inside the United States without acquiring court-approved search warrants normally required for domestic spying. The president explained that the program was necessary after 9/11 in order to rapidly monitor the phone calls and

President George W. Bush bows his head in prayer. Bush and his supporters believe that God is on the side of the U.S. in the war against terror.

other communications of people in the United States who may have contact with al Qaeda and other terrorist groups. Critics charged, however, that the Pentagon used the program to collect information on peaceful activists and antiwar protesters. Regardless of these criticisms, Congress reauthorized the Patriot Act on March 9, 2006, with only minor changes.

Similar concerns have been raised about antiterrorism security measures adopted by other countries. Amnesty International, a human rights organization, warns:

In the name of fighting "international terrorism," governments have rushed to introduce draconian new measures that threaten the human rights of their own citizens, immigrants and refugees. . . . Governments have a responsibility to ensure the safety of their citizens, but measures taken must not undermine fundamental human rights standards. It appears that some of the initiatives currently being discussed or implemented may be used to curb basic human rights and to suppress internal opposition. Some of the definitions of "terrorism" under discussion are so broad that they could be used to criminalize anyone out of favour with those in power and criminalize legitimate peaceful exercise of the right to freedom of expression and association. They could also put at risk the right to privacy and threaten the rights of minorities and asylum-seekers.[51]

Experts say that striking the right balance between national security and civil liberties will be a delicate challenge. So far, although a growing number of people are concerned about a loss of their civil liberties, polls show that a slim majority of the American public is willing to accept warrantless surveillance as a necessary evil to keep America safe from suicide terrorist attacks. A thin majority of Americans also continues to support other parts of the U.S. war on terror. Unless this public support declines, most observers expect the costs of the war on terror in the United States, both monetary and otherwise, to continue to mount.

Chapter Five

Stopping Suicide Terror

Experts and policy makers are divided over the best strategies for combating suicide terrorism. Before September 11, 2001, most countries routinely handled terrorist attacks as law enforcement and criminal justice matters. Since the 9/11 tragedy, however, the United States and some other nations have opted for a military response, coupled with various other strategies in an American-led war on terror. Whether this war will be successful in containing or reducing today's growing phenomenon of suicide bombings has yet to be determined.

Law Enforcement

One widespread approach to fighting terrorism, including suicide bombings, is a legal one that employs the tools of law enforcement and criminal justice. Before September 11, in fact, this was the main strategy used by the United States and most other countries in fighting both domestic and global terrorism. The FBI, the investigative arm of the U.S. Justice Department and the lead federal agency for counterterrorism, was charged with preventing and prosecuting terrorism in the United States.

In America, this law enforcement system produced a number of successes. Between 1993 until 2002, for example, the United States prosecuted several major international terrorism cases. U.S. officials were successful in convicting six al Qaeda defendants responsible for the 1993 bombing of the World Trade Center, another six al Qaeda defendants for their involvement in a 1998 bombing of U.S. embassies in East Africa, and more than a dozen other defendants for their roles in two failed terrorist plots against the United States. Osama bin Laden himself, the leader of the al Qaeda terrorist network, was indicted long before September 11—for conspiring to kill Americans and for the bombings of U.S. embassies in Nairobi, Kenya, and Dar es Salaam, Tanzania, in 1998. Also, in August 2001, Algerian Ahmed Ressam, a terrorist trained by al Qaeda who planned a truck bombing of the Los Angeles International Airport just before the millennium New Year's Eve, was convicted along with two helpers.

Investigations following the September 11 attack, however, revealed deep flaws in this system. Investigators, for example, discovered that the FBI mishandled key leads that could potentially have uncovered and prevented the September 11 attack. One widely publicized mistake, for example, was the refusal to authorize a wiretap and search of the computer records of Zacarias Moussaoui, a French Moroccan arrested before September 11 and now believed to have been a member of the September 11 conspiracy. If such a search had been authorized, authorities might have found data about cockpit layouts of commercial air-

This suicide bomber was caught before she was able to carry out her terrorist act.

craft and phone numbers that could have led them to the other members of the September 11 plot. The post–September 11 criticisms led to reforms at the FBI and promises that the FBI would coordinate more closely with the Central Intelligence Agency (CIA), the U.S. agency that collects intelligence on terrorists abroad. Also, under the Patriot Act, FBI agents were given vast new investigative and surveillance powers. Finally, in December 2004, a new law—the Intelligence Reform and Terrorism Prevention Act—was enacted to officially reorganize and reform the entire U.S. intelligence system.

After September 11, many terrorism experts still see the value in the law enforcement approach, particularly for prosecuting small-scale operations or organizations that have hierarchical systems where leaders can be identified and arrested. These small groups can be investigated and their operations degraded by the arrest and prosecution of their leaders and by following their money trails. Also, treating terrorists like common criminals, some experts believe, prevents them from gaining political legitimacy, often one of the terrorists' main goals. As former FBI agent Michael German explains, "By treating terrorists like criminals, we stigmatize them in their own community, while simultaneously validating our own authority. Open and public trials allow the community to see the terrorist for the criminal he is, and successful prosecutions give them faith their government is protecting them."[52] However, because terrorism is now understood as a major in-

The Moroccan nationalist Zacarias Moussaoui was arrested before the 9/11 attacks but is believed to be part of the terrorist conspiracy.

ternational threat, bolder and more global strategies have also become increasingly popular.

Military Strategies

After September 11, for example, the United States adopted a robust new military strategy against al Qaeda terror, even calling it a "war" on terror. The U.S. offensive in Afghanistan was waged to deny al Qaeda a sanctuary, and Iraq was invaded to oust its leader, Saddam Hussein, based on charges that he was developing weapons of mass destruction. Today, after anti-American terrorist insurgencies have arisen in both countries, U.S. policy makers claim that the wars in Afghanistan and Iraq are an even more critical part of the U.S. antiterror campaign. President Bush now emphasizes the importance of engaging the terrorists abroad rather than at home and calls Iraq "the central front for the war on terror."[53] As Bush explained in August 2004:

On September the 11th, 2001, we saw the future that the terrorists intend for our country and the lengths they're willing to go to achieve their aims. We faced a clear choice. We could hunker down, retreating behind a false sense of security, or we could bring the war to the terrorists, striking them before they could kill more of our people. I made a decision—America will not wait to be attacked again. Our doctrine is clear: We will confront emerging threats before they fully materialize. And if you harbor a terrorist, you're just as guilty as the terrorist. We will stay on the offense. We'll complete our work in Afghanistan and Iraq. An immediate withdrawal of our troops in Iraq, or the broader Middle East, as some have called for, would only embolden the terrorists and create a staging ground to launch more attacks against America and free nations. So long as I'm the President, we will stay, we will fight, and we will win the war on terror.[54]

Supporters of an offensive military approach hope to make it difficult or impossible for terrorist groups to continue to do business. Covert military action, for example, can be used to conduct surgical attacks on terrorist headquarters or training facilities and to arrest or kill militant leaders who are suspected of planning or promoting terrorist strikes. Such actions can eliminate terrorist leadership and disrupt critical terrorist operations such as funding, training, recruitment, planning, publicity, and propaganda.

Efforts to crush terrorist groups militarily is a strategy embraced by other nations as well. Israel, for example, has long been known for pursuing an ironfisted military strategy against Palestinian terror groups. The Israeli military has put down Palestinian protests and uprisings with overwhelming military force and has long enforced strict curfew and travel restrictions on Palestinian civilians in the hopes of suppressing and detecting terrorists. Following a suicide attack, Israel routinely bulldozes the suicide bomber's family home, and in recent years, the Israeli military has developed a policy of assassinating militant leaders in an attempt to disrupt Hamas and other Palestinian terrorist groups. Israel attributes the recent reduction in Palestinian suicide attacks, beginning in 2004, partly to its policy of killing or capturing many of the militant Hamas and other terrorist group leaders.

The Sri Lankan government has also followed a military strategy in its effort to eliminate Tamil suicide terrorism. The government responded to Tamil suicide bomb attacks with curfews, police harassment, and repression in Tamil communities. Troops sent into Tamil areas destroyed homes and farms, subjected civilians to ex-

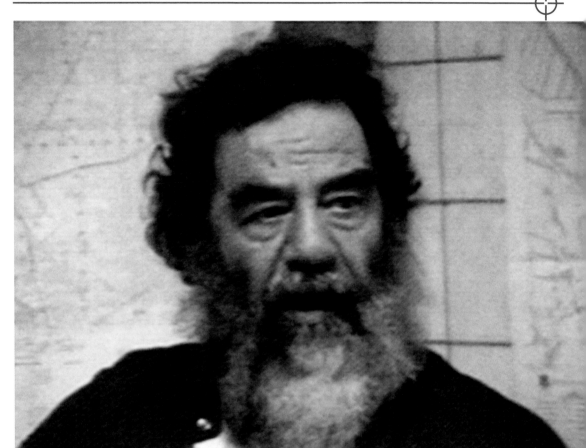

Iraq's government crumbled after U.S. troops ousted Saddam Hussein, shown here after his capture and arrest..

ecutions, rapes, and torture, and used overwhelming force to try to subdue the rebels. The Sri Lankan government has hailed this hard-line military approach as the only way to bring peace to the country.

Another nation that takes a hard-line approach to suicide terror is Russia. For years, Russian soldiers routinely raped and tortured Chechen civilians and looted their villages. These tactics—although not officially sanctioned by the Russian government —have largely destroyed Chechnya's cities, economy, and society. Since the Chechens began using suicide and other terrorist methods in recent years, the Russian government has strengthened its tough military policy and sought to further increase government power and security, all in the name of fighting terrorism. In 2005, for example, Russian president Vladimir Putin announced that the federal government, instead of local voters, will choose the regional governors. He also proposed legislation to strengthen the state security forces, restrict the movement of citizens within Russia, and enlist citizens to spy on fellow citizens. Putin and his supporters believe that this authoritarian approach is justified in order to respond to terrorism and prevent the country from being torn apart by the Chechen separatists.

Many terrorism experts, however, charge that while military responses to terrorism sometimes bring temporary victories, they often fail in the long run to end suicide attacks. Palestinian groups, for example, have often simply regrouped and increased terrorist strikes after harsh Israeli military crackdowns and assassinations. Terrorism in Sri Lanka also seemed to intensify after the government, seeking to defeat the Tamils militarily, sent troops into

Tamil areas. In Russia, too, many observers say that the government's aggressive military strategy against the Chechens has only escalated that insurgency, making it more desperate, extreme, and apt to use suicide terrorism. In addition, critics say, the authoritarian Russian antiterror approach is rapidly moving the country away from democracy and toward a police state like that which existed under communist dictators in the former Soviet Union.

Similarly, many terrorism experts and political analysts claim that the U.S. invasions of Afghanistan and Iraq have strengthened al Qaeda and created more rather than less terrorism in that region and the world. Those who study terrorism point out that al Qaeda's leader, Osama bin

 ## Germany's Approach to Terrorism

After September 11, some countries chose not to respond to terrorism with military means. Germany, for example, expressed its strong support for America after 9/11 but opted to limit its antiterrorism efforts to a legalistic approach. German leaders see terrorism fundamentally as a violation of German and international laws of war that prohibit the targeting of noncombatant civilians and similar atrocities. Instead of joining American forces in military actions in Afghanistan and Iraq, Germany passed legislation to reform existing antiterrorism laws and provide more funding for identifying and prosecuting terrorists. One big

change in the law, for example, allowed German law enforcement to go after terrorist groups operating anywhere in the European Union and, under certain conditions, even groups outside of Europe. Germany also expanded the surveillance and information-gathering capabilities of its law enforcement agencies, but it placed many limits on these activities. Germany's experience of government abuse of power by the Nazis during World War II has made it cautious in expanding police powers. Altogether, German efforts have led to a number of impressive successes, including convictions of several high-level al Qaeda operatives.

Vladimir Putin speaks in front of a patriotic Russian background. Putin's government employs tough military tactics against Chechens and other ethnic groups.

Laden is still alive, and that the group's decentralized structure since the U.S. attacks has made its operations tougher to disrupt. Also, al Qaeda seems to have a continuing and perhaps growing ability to attract legions of fighters, supporters, and sympathizers around the world. As Jessica Stern suggests, "Whenever we respond with violence of any kind, we assist the terrorists in mobilizing recruits."[55]

Indeed, al Qaeda's ability to stage terrorist strikes appears to have actually increased since 2001. As former government terrorism expert Richard A. Clarke explained in congressional testimony in 2004, "There have been more major al Qaeda related attacks globally in the 30 months since 9-11 than there were in the 30 months preceding it. Hostility toward the US in the

Islamic world has increased since 9-11, largely as a result of the invasion and occupation of Iraq."[56]

Intelligence, Financial, and WMD Strategies

Today, there is a growing consensus that a variety of strategies must be employed in the war on terror. Military action, for example, does not rule out the simultaneous use of other tactics. An emphasis on intelligence and surveillance—long the tools of law enforcement—is considered especially critical by many experts. By monitoring communications and infiltrating close-knit terrorist organizations with spies, antiterrorism agents can sometimes discover and thwart terror plots before they are implemented. Former FBI agent Michael

German explains what he learned from infiltrating terrorist groups: "The one thing that stopped terrorists from following through on their plans was the fear that they had been compromised by an infiltrator. If the terrorist knows that every new recruit is a possible agent; if every old friend might have turned; if communications over the phone, or over the radio, or over the internet are vulnerable to interception, his ability to operate effectively is greatly restricted."[57] Accurate intelligence also allows governments to understand how a terrorist organization functions, who is making the decisions, and how best to undercut the group's effectiveness.

Financial strategies designed to track and freeze monetary donations and support of terrorist organizations are another important law enforcement tool. As Gerald P. O'Driscoll Jr., Brett D. Schaefer, and John C. Hulsman of the Heritage Foundation explain, "Osama bin Laden is a modern financier dedicated to supporting terrorist acts through a complex financial network. A multimillionaire, he utilizes not only his own resources, but also money that flows in from supporters around the world, rich and poor. As a sort of diabolical grant maker, he distributes funds to groups that are planning to harm Western and particularly American interests."[58] By cutting off or curtailing the movement of funds, authorities can deny terrorists access to their international financial support, thus disrupting their terror activities.

Necessary, too, are diplomatic and political strategies. After September 11, 2001, many countries joined the United States in its antiterrorism drive and in recent years U.S. government agencies have frequently consulted with foreign governments to share intelligence information and coordinate antiterror strategies. In many cases, this has led to the arrests of dangerous terrorists who otherwise may not have been caught. A number of conferences have also been held to explore better ways to create a global approach to terrorism and the

American actions in Iraq and Afghanistan have not eliminated the terrorist threat, but some al Qaeda leaders, such as Abu Musab al-Zarqawi, have been killed by U.S. forces.

Osama bin Laden, shown here (on the left) with an advisor, is a prime source of financial support for al Qaeda. Part of U.S. strategy includes cutting off terrorist funds.

trend is toward even greater international cooperation in the future.

One important part of this international approach to terror is the effort to control the global distribution of weapons of mass destruction (WMD)—nuclear, chemical, and biological weapons—that suicide terrorists could use for ever more destructive attacks. Several developments suggest that terrorists may soon use such weapons against civilian targets. First, WMD are especially useful in killing large numbers of people and producing widespread terror, the goal of many modern terrorists. Also, nuclear weapons and technology are more readily available now on the black market due to the collapse of the Soviet Union, and nations like North Korea are exporting equipment that can be used to make chemical and biological weapons. Finally, technological advances such as the Internet help terrorist groups communicate with and educate sympathizers about terrorist goals and WMD technology. As Jessica Stern explains, "[WMD terrorism's] expected cost—in lives lost and in threats to civil liberties—is potentially devastating. Government officials will be remiss—and will be blamed—if they do not take measures to reduce the likelihood and severity of the threat."[59]

Since 9/11, the U.S. government has claimed success against al Qaeda using such a combination of military, law enforcement, and other strategies. In a 2003 report, for example, the Bush administration stated that the government had arrested or killed nearly two-thirds of al Qaeda's leaders, either convicted or obtained guilty pleas from over 140 terrorists, and denied terrorist networks over $200 million in funds. More recently, on October 6, 2005, President Bush said that U.S. authorities have prevented at least ten serious al Qaeda terrorist plots since September 11, including three attempts to attack inside the United States.

In addition, since 9/11, countries around the world are cooperating with each other on an unprecedented basis and many are touting their own successes. German, Italian, French, Spanish, Dutch, and British police have broken up al Qaeda cells and secured several major convictions. European countries also have worked to stop nuclear smuggling, helping to expose Abdul Khadeer Khan, the father of Pakistan's atomic bomb, as a seller of nuclear secrets to Libya, Iran, and North Korea—a major victory. Pressure on Libya, in turn, led Libya's leaders to renounce support for terrorism and weapons of mass destruction. Even some Muslim countries that once supported terrorism have come to realize that al Qaeda terrorism is a threat and have

begun expanding their anti terrorism efforts. Pakistan, for example, has arrested dozens of Islamist radicals who are suspected of plotting suicide attacks. Saudi Arabia, too, has disrupted al Qaeda cells and improved its law enforcement operations against terrorism.

Fighting Root Causes of Terrorism

Despite some measurable successes in the global fight against terrorism, many terrorism experts and policy makers believe that it is critical to try to eradicate the root causes of suicide terrorism. Some have urged, for example, that it is important to provide economic aid and education to poor communities to lift up people who feel so despairing about their place in the world that they resort to terrorism. This strategy, some claim, worked well in Turkey, which was wracked by suicide bombings conducted by a Kurdish rebel group, the PKK, in the mid-1990s. Besides staging military attacks on rebel bases and arresting the PKK leader, the Turkish government worked to improve the living conditions of the local civilian population. The government helped create stable governing processes, agreed to Kurdish demands for language and cultural freedoms, and funded social-welfare programs to improve agriculture and education. In addition, the Turkish government invested over $32 billion in the Kurdish southeast region, transforming its economy. These efforts, some experts say, helped to virtually eliminate suicide terrorism in Turkey.

Pakistanis protest the jailing of Abdul Khadeer Khan (pictured in the poster) and other scientists accused of selling nuclear secrets.

Other scholars have stressed promoting democracy and freedom as a major part of the answer to terrorism. As German journalist Christoph Reuter puts it, "The war that must be fought is one that destroys, from the inside out, the reasons for a phenomenon such as Bin Laden. It must be a war for democracy, freedom, human rights—and for institutions that protect, defend and consolidate these values. . . . Only a war such as this—against oppression and injustice . . . —can destroy terrorism."[60] The Bush administration, embracing this view, argues that it is vital to establish, support, and defend democratic governments in Iraq and Afghanistan to prevent them from being taken over by terrorist extremists. The United States also has lobbied for greater political freedoms in other Middle Eastern nations, including hostile countries like Iran as well as U.S. allies such as Saudi Arabia, Jordan, and Egypt.

Another proposed strategy is for governments to examine the political grievances of terrorist groups and consider changing government policies in ways that might address those grievances. Some experts say that today's Islamic terrorism is directed at U.S. policies that are viewed as arrogant, hypocritical, and hurtful. As terrorism expert Jessica Stern explains:

The answer to the question "Why do they hate us?" is not only the [envy] inevitably engendered by our military and economic might, but also our policies. . . . It is not just who they are and not just who we are, but also, at least in part, what we do. We station troops in restive regions, engendering popular resentment. We maintained ineffective sanctions against Iraq, generating widespread outrage at their effect on Iraqi citizens. We demand that other countries adhere to international law, but willfully and shortsightedly weaken instruments that we perceive as not advancing our current needs. . . . We look the other way when Israel violates human rights. . . . We demand that other countries open their markets to our goods, even as we maintain protections on ours. . . . In short, we need to take into account how our policies play into the hands of our terrorist enemies.[61]

History professor Thomas R. Mockaitis argues that the United States and other countries must win the trust of the general population that supports the extremists. This can happen, Mockaitis says, only if governments recognize and try to address "the real needs and the legitimate grievances on which the insurgency feeds."[62] This strategy, Mockaitis argues, does not give in to terrorism. It simply provides another potentially effective weapon in the antiterrorism toolbox.

To combat the growing trend of Islamic terrorism against U.S. and other Western targets, for example, Mockaitis urges the United States to move toward a more balanced foreign policy that avoids unilateral actions such as the war in Iraq. He also suggests modifying U.S. support

Winning the Battle for Hearts and Minds

Terrorism expert Scott Atran says that the most effective policy to counter Muslim terrorists is one that seeks to eliminate the community support that terrorist groups require to survive and thrive. According to Atran, policy makers must first identify and try to address the real or imagined grievances of terrorist groups. These grievances determine the goals for which volunteers are asked to sacrifice themselves in suicide bombings. Islamist terrorist groups often turn such grievances into sacred values by infusing them with religious significance. Next, Atran argues that U.S. funds should be redirected to compete for the people's

support by building quality schools and providing medical and social services to Muslim regions. Because governments in these regions fail to answer these needs, terrorist groups step in to finance radical Islamist schools and other services that create support for terror. Replacing radical programs with moderate ones, Atran says, would reduce the pool of suicide bomber volunteers. Finally, Atran says that the United States should support economic and political freedom in the Muslim world and withdraw military and political support from Arab governments that infringe on human rights or deny political expression.

---

for Israel by being more sympathetic to the plight of the Palestinians in order to produce an acceptable resolution of the Israeli-Palestinian conflict.

The problem with this approach is that groups using suicide tactics have many different motivations and political demands and operate in various locations, under the direction of many different leaders. In many cases, too, the demands of suicide terrorist groups are so extreme, or their actions so violent, that the governments that have been attacked refuse to negotiate or change their policies until the suicide terrorism stops. In the Arab-Israeli conflict, for example, Israel and its ally, the United States, are currently reluctant to negotiate with

Hamas, the winner of recent Palestinian parliamentary elections, until Hamas renounces its call for the destruction of Israel and its use of suicide and terrorist violence.

In the end, most experts seem to agree that there is no single way to eliminate the threat of suicide terrorism in modern society, only a range of options, each of which has its place depending on ever-changing circumstances and realities. Faced with this threat, governments have no other choice but to commit to a long-term antiterrorism struggle. As political commentators David Frum and Richard Perle put it, "Terrorism remains the great evil of our time, and the war against this evil, our generation's great cause."[63]

Notes

Chapter 1: The Problem of Suicide Terrorists

1. Quoted in Council on Foreign Relations, "Terrorism: Questions & Answers: Hamas," 2004. http://cfrterrorism.org/ groups/ hamas.html.

2. Quoted in John Vause, "Israeli Youth: 'I Don't Want to Die Today,'" CNN.com, June 28, 2002. http://archives.cnn.com /2002/WORLD/meast/06/28/vot.terror. five/.

3. Quoted in Mandi Steele, "Survivors Face Agony in Suicide Attacks," WorldNetDaily. com, May 30, 2002. www.worldnetdaily. com/news/article.asp?ARTICLE_ID=27778.

4. Christoph Reuter, "*My Life Is a Weapon: A Modern History of Suicide Bombing.* Princeton, NJ: Princeton University Press, 2005, p. 161.

5. Sharif Abdullah, "Avoiding a Generation of Terrorism: Lessons from Sri Lanka," Peacework, March 2002. www.afsc.org/ pwork/0203/020318.htm.

6. Council on Foreign Relations, "Terrorism: Questions & Answers: Al-Qaeda," July 2005. http://cfrterrorism.org/groups/ alqaeda.html.

7. Quoted in Council on Foreign Relations, "Terrorism: Questions & Answers: Osama bin Laden: Al-Qaeda Leader," February 2006. http://cfr.org/publication/9951/.

8. Andrew Silke, "Profiling Terror," *Police Review*, August 7, 2003.

9. Robert L. DuPont, Elizabeth DuPont Spencer, and Caroline M. DuPont, "Terrorism: Anxiety on a Global Scale," American Council on Science and Health, December 3, 2002. www.acsh.org/health issues/newsID.463/healthissue_detail.asp.

Chapter 2: What Motivates Suicide Bombers?

10. Scott Atran, "Genesis of Suicide Terrorism," *Science*, March 7, 2003, p. 1534.

11. Quoted in John Gray, "From Drifters to Warriors," *New Statesman*, September 12, 2005, p. 48. Reprinted at www.looks marttrends.com/p/articles/mi_m0FQP/is _4757_134/ai_n15863267#continue.

12. Quoted in Bruce Hoffman, "The Logic of Suicide Terrorism," *Atlantic Monthly*, June 2003, p. 40.

13. Quoted in Michael Bond, "The Making of a Suicide Bomber: What Drives Someone to Kill Themselves While Killing Others?" *New Scientist*, May 15, 2004, p. 34.

14. Quoted in Georgie Anne Geyer, "Suicide Bombers as Political Weapons," *Chicago Tribune*, June 17, 2005. Reprinted at http://list.nowar-paix.ca/pipermail/no war/2005-June/000707.html.

15. Mia Bloom, *Dying to Kill: The Allure of Suicide Terror.* New York: Columbia University Press, 2005, p. 36.

16. Quoted in Frank Warner, "Harvard's Alberto Albadie on the Solution to Terrorism: It's Freedom, Stupid," November 9, 2004. http://frankwarner.typepad.

com/free_frank_warner/2004/11/harvards_albert.html.

17. Alan B. Krueger and Jitka Maleckova, "Education, Poverty, and Terrorism: Is There a Connection?" *Journal of Economic Perspectives*, Fall 2003, p. 119.

18. Krueger and Maleckova, "Education, Poverty, and Terrorism."

19. Baruch Kimmerling, "Sacred Rage," *Nation*, December 15, 2003, p. 23.

20. Quoted in Kimmerling, "Sacred Rage." p. 23.

21. Jessica Stern, *Terror in the Name of God*. New York: HarperCollins, 2003, p. 285.

22. Quoted in Stern, *Terror in the Name of God*, p. 216.

23. Stefan Lovgren, "Suicide Attacks Evolving, Increasing," National Geographic News, July 29, 2005. http://news.nationalgeographic.com/news/2005/07/0729_050729_suicide.html.

24. Quoted in Lionel Beehner, "Iraq: Suicide Attacks," Council on Foreign Relations, August 1, 2005. www.cfr.org/publication/8583/iraq.html?jsessionid=366f069c75305cdb7844113fb2b0eaad.

25. Stern, *Terror in the Name of God*, pp. 282–83.

26. Marc Sageman, *Understanding Terror Networks*. Philadelphia: University of Pennsylvania Press, 2004, p. 1.

27. Bloom, *Dying to Kill*, p. 88.

28. Quoted in Ewen MacAskill, "The Suicide Bomber Is the Smartest of Smart Bombs," *Guardian*, July 14, 2005. www.guardian.co.uk/israel/Story/0,2763,1528098,00.html.

29. Quoted in Scott McConnell, "The Logic of Suicide Terrorism," *American Conservative*, July 18, 2005. www.amconmag.com/2005_07_18/article.html.

30. Quoted in McConnell, "Logic of Suicide Terrorism."

31. Quoted in McConnell, "Logic of Suicide Terrorism."

Chapter 3: How Is Suicide Terrorism Justified?

32. Quoted in KABC-TV, "Britain's Largest Sunni Group Condemns London Bombings," July 14, 2005. http://abclocal.go.com/kabc/story?section=news&id=3259189.

33. Quoted in John Kelsay, "Suicide Bombers: The 'Just War' Debate," *Christian Century*, August 14–27, 2002, pp. 22–25. www.religion-online.org/showarticle.asp?title=2616.

34. Quoted in Associated Press, "Moderate Muslims Split on Suicide Bombings," Fox News, July 20, 2005. www.foxnews.com/story/0,2933,163075,00.html.

35. Eyad Sarraj, "Why We Blow Ourselves Up," *Time*, April 8, 2004. www.time.com/time/covers/1101020408/viewpoint.html.

36. Chandra Muzaffar, "Suicide Bombing: Is Another Form of Struggle Possible?" Media Review Network, May 31, 2002. www.mediareviewnet.com/Suicide%20Bombing%20by%20muzaffar.htm.

37. Stern, *Terror in the Name of God*, p. 282.

38. Quoted in Reuter, *My Life Is a Weapon*, p. 114.

39. Quoted in Martin Kramer, "The Moral Logic of Hizballah," in *Origins of Terrorism: Psychologies, Ideologies, Theologies, States of Mind*, ed. Walter Reich. Cam-

bridge: Cambridge University Press, 1990, pp. 131–57.

40. Quoted in Bloom, *Dying to Kill*, pp. 3–4.

41. *The Estimate*, "Suicide Bombing As a Problem in Asymmetric Warfare," April 9, 2003. www.theestimate.com/public/041902.html.

42. Quoted in McConnell, "Logic of Suicide Terrorism."

43. Ramzi Kysia, "Towards a Nonviolent Resistance in Palestine," *Jordan Times*, April 23, 2004. Reprinted at http://middleeast info.org/article.php?sid=652.

Chapter 4: The Costs of Suicide Terrorism

44. James Bovard, *Terrorism and Tyranny*, New York: Palgrave MacMillan, 2003, p. 350.

45. American Psychological Association Task Force on Promoting Resilience in Response to Terrorism, "Fostering Resilience in Response to Terrorism: A Fact Sheet for Psychologists Working with Adults," 2005. www.apa.org/psychologists/pdfs/adults.pdf.

46. Flore de Préneuf, "Living with Terrorism," Salon.com, September 13, 2001. www.salon.com/politics/feature/2001/09/13/israel/.

47. Quoted in Stephen Gale, "Hurricane Katrina and Terrorism," Foreign Policy Research Institute, September 8, 2005. www. fpri.org/enotes/20050908.amer ica war.gale.hurricanekatrinaterrorism. html.

48. Quoted in James Gordon Meek and Maki Becker, "Security Comes at High Cost," *New York Daily News*, May 1, 2005. Reprinted at www.globalsecurity.org/org/news/2005/050508-security-cost.htm.

49. American Civil Liberties Union, "The USA PATRIOT ACT and Government Actions That Threaten Our Civil Liberties," February 11, 2003. www.aclu.org/takeaction/general/18880pub20030211.html#attach.

50. George W. Bush, speech at Ohio State Highway Patrol Academy, Columbus, Ohio, June 9, 2005. www.whitehouse.gov/news/releases/2005/06/20050609-2.html.

51. Amnesty International, "The Backlash: Human Rights at Risk Around the World," October 4, 2001. http://web.amnesty.org/library/index/engACT30027 2001?OpenDocument.

Chapter 5: Stopping Suicide Terror

52. Michael German, "Squaring the Error," *Conference Report: Law vs. War: Competing Approaches to Fighting Terrorism*, Strategic Studies Institute, July 2005. www.globalsecurity.org/security/library/report/2005/pub613.pdf.

53. White House, *Progress Report on the Global War on Terrorism*, September 2003, p. 4. www.whitehouse.gov/homeland/progress/progress_report_0903.pdf.

54. George W. Bush, speech to military families in Nampa, Idaho, August 24, 2005. www.whitehouse.gov/news/releases/2005/08/20050824.html.

55. Stern, *Terror in the Name of God*, p. 289.

56. Quoted in Bloom, *Dying to Kill*, p. 182.

57. German, "Squaring the Error."

58. Gerald P. O'Driscoll Jr., Brett D. Schaefer, and John C. Hulsman, "Stopping

Terrorism: Follow the Money," Heritage Foundation, September 25, 2001. www.heritage.org/Research/NationalSecurity/BG1479.cfm.

59. Jessica Stern, *The Ultimate Terrorists*. Cambridge, MA: Harvard University Press, 1999, p. 10.

60. Reuter, *My Life Is a Weapon*, pp. 178–79.

61. Stern, *Terror in the Name of God*, pp. 294–95.

62. Thomas R. Mockaitis, "Winning Hearts and Minds in the 'War on Terrorism,'" in *Grand Strategy in the War Against Terrorism*, ed. Thomas R. Mockaitis and Paul B. Rich. Portland, OR: Frank Cass, 2003, p. 21.

63. Quoted in James Bovard, "The Neocon War on Peace and Freedom," Future of Freedom Foundation, February 21, 2004. www.antiwar.com/orig2/bovard022104.html.

For Further Reading

Books

Sandra Donovan, *Protecting America: A Look at the People Who Keep Our Country Safe.* Minneapolis: Lerner, 2004. A young adult book about the U.S. armed forces, border guards, health officials, and others who help to keep Americans safe from terrorism and other dangers.

Fiona MacDonald, *The September 11th Terrorist Attacks.* Milwaukee: World Almanac Library, 2004. Describes the causes, events, people, and legacy of the September 11 terrorist attacks.

Phillip Margulies, *Al Qaeda: Osama bin Laden's Army of Terrorists.* New York: Rosen, 2003. An overview of the Islamic terrorist group al Qaeda and its role in the September 11 terrorist attacks in the United States.

Periodicals

Aparisim Ghosh, "Professor of Death: An Iraqi Insurgent Leader Reveals How He Trains and Equips Suicide Bombers and Sends Them on Their Lethal Missions," *Time*, October 24, 2005.

Bruce Hoffman, "The Logic of Suicide Terrorism," *Atlantic Monthly*, June 2003.

Amanda Ripley, "Why Suicide Bombing . . . Is Now All the Rage," *Time*, April 15, 2002.

Lee Kuan Yew, "Homegrown Islamic Terrorists," *Forbes*, October 17, 2005.

Mortimer B. Zuckerman, "In for the Grim Long Haul," *U.S. News & World Report*, June 14, 2004.

Web Sites

American Civil Liberties Union (ACLU) (www.aclu.org/about/index.html). This Web site run by the country's most well-known private and nonpartisan civil liberties organization provides detailed information about the Patriot Act and efforts to renew the legislation.

Council on Foreign Relations, "Terrorism: Questions & Answers (http://cfrterrorism.org/home/). A very informative Web site offering information about the various types of terrorism (including suicide bombings), terrorist groups worldwide, and the U.S. responses following the attacks on September 11, 2001.

Federal Bureau of Investigation (FBI) (www.fbi.gov/terrorinfo/counterrorism/waronterrorhome.htm). A federal law enforcement Web site that provides information about terrorism as well as pictures and descriptions of the agency's most wanted terrorists.

Institute of Peace and Conflict Studies, "IPCS Program on Suicide Terrorism" (www.suicideterrorism.org/). A Web site run by an independent think tank located in India that features up-to-date information about suicide terrorist campaigns in various areas around the world.

U.S. Department of State Counterterrorism Office (www.state.gov/s/ct/). A government Web site on counterterrorism that offers an overview of U.S. efforts to combat terrorism, annual reports on global terrorism patterns, and travel alerts.

Index

Picture Credits

Cover: © Reuters/CORBIS
© AFP/Getty Images, 25
© Akram Saleh/Reuters/CORBIS, 13
© Anuruddha Lokuhapuarachchi/Reuters/CORBIS, 34
© Asim Tanveer/Reuters/CORBIS, 77
© Brooks Kraft/CORBIS, 65
© Ed Kashi/CORBIS, 22
© Getty Images, 11
© Handout/Reuters/CORBIS, 27, 36, 71
© Howard Davies/CORBIS, 20
© Hulton Archive/Getty Images, 12
© John D. McHugh/Getty Images, 38
© Kai Pfaffenbach/Reuters/CORBIS, 51
© Maggie Hallahan/CORBIS, 56-57
© Mashkov Yuri/ITAR-TASS/CORBIS, 50
Maury Aaseng, 18
© Maxim Marmur-Pool/epa/CORBIS, 73
© Patrick Chauvel/Sygma/CORBIS, 17
© Peter Macdiarmid/epa/CORBIS, 42
© Peter Turnley/CORBIS, 33, 54
© Peter Turnley/The Denver Post/CORBIS, 58
© PETRA/Reuters/CORBIS, 74
© Reuters/CORBIS, 30, 31, 48, 60, 64, 69, 75
© REUTERS TV/Reuters/CORBIS, 44, 46
© Reza; Webistan/CORBIS, 16
© Rob Howard/CORBIS, 24
© RONEN ZVULUN/Reuters/CORBIS, 68
© Shaul Schwarz/CORBIS, 63

About the Author

Debra A. Miller is a writer and lawyer with a passion for current events and history. She began her law career in Washington, D.C., where she worked on legislative, policy, and legal matters in government, public interest, and private law firm positions. She now lives with her husband in Encinitas, California where she writes and edits books and anthologies on historical, political, and other topics.